LIFE ON THE HILL

Be-Attitudes for Everyday Life

Chris Spicer

malcolm down

PUBLISHING

Cover design by Luther Spicer
Line drawings by Taffy Davies

Printed in the UK

BY THE SAME AUTHOR

No Perfect Fathers Here
JJ & the Big Bend
The Reel Story

DEDICATION

To Winnie, a godly mother,
last seen heading for the top.

RECOMMENDATIONS

"*Life on the Hill* lifts us to the summit of a sun-soaked mountain two thousand years ago. Through Chris's lucid prose, we hear with a new clarity and understand with a new urgency the most important message ever preached – Jesus's Sermon on the Mount. If you're looking for a book to give you a lift in your relationship with God and with others, this is it. So, fasten your straps and prepare for the ascent; reading *Life on the Hill* is truly a mountain-top experience. It comes from an altitude where you breathe the pure oxygen of revival."

Dr Mark Stibbe
Award-winning author, and founder of www.thebooklab.co.uk

"I first heard Chris teach the core principles he so delightfully weaves together in this book, about thirty years ago. They have since been honed and proven in the furnace of life and the result is a superbly written, must-read book for every serious disciple of Jesus. It is a guidebook for all who are tired of mediocrity, want to live life at a higher level and are committed to helping Christianity find its voice of hope in our sin-sick world."

Stephen Matthew
Pastor, teacher, author, coach and committed church-builder, Bradford, UK

"If you thought this book would turn out to be another gentle, honey-coated devotional text on the beatitudes you will soon discover this is a wrong assumption. This is a strong book; it is a thought-provoking and stimulating read. I found it challenging and heart engaging. Chris Spicer is a master storyteller and uses story and allegory to apply his message in practical and powerful ways. I highly commend it to those ready to lift their vision and take the ascent to the highest level of Christian discipleship."

Revd Ian Jennings
Associate Minister, St Mary's, Denham, Buckinghamshire, UK

"Drawing from deep wells, the experience of life, the example of others and above all the radical teaching of Jesus Christ, this book challenges to the core what it means to live a Kingdom lifestyle this side of eternity. It corrects misconceptions and induces a hunger for more of God in our shallow and desperate world.

"Chris is a wordsmith creatively painting vivid pictures that make you think deeply about yourself and the Saviour he clearly knows intimately. Some books inform the mind, which is good; others stir the emotions, which is necessary; and still others feed the soul and fire the spirit, which is essential. This book does all of that. Read, learn, weep, laugh, sing, act and change."

Steve Campbell
Senior Pastor, The C3 Church, Cambridge, UK

"This book is rich, a tapestry, a mosaic, and a work of art, history, and prophecy all wrapped up in one. Chris has transformed the timeless Sermon on the Mount into a handbook for today. And today, of course, is not just any day but a moment of need, opportunity and challenge.

"Chris's ability to evoke hunger, harness desperation, envision the adventurer, and birth the world-changer is evident throughout this book. It is great for the individual reader, ideal for small groups, and it has the quality of genius."

Paul Manwaring
Member Senior Leadership Team, Bethel Church, California

"The skill of a great Bible teacher is to reignite the fire that is in words written 2000 years ago for this generation. To bring relevance, challenge and encouragement to those who seek to hear God speaking. Chris does this brilliantly in his latest book *Life on the Hill*. Having read it I wonder if I should read it every year to remind me of what Jesus taught. A relevant look at an ancient text."

Mark Jarvis
Management Consultant, Hunmoco Business Consultancy, UK

ACKNOWLEDGEMENTS

First and foremost, I would like to give my heartfelt thanks to my wife Tina. Without her love, patience and constant companionship over the last fifty years, the necessary attitude change in my life would never have been made possible. I am also sincerely grateful to Mark Stibbe and the good folks at BookLab (www.thebooklab.co.uk) for their editorial expertise. Without their work, this publication would probably never have seen the light of day. A big thank you to Malcolm Down and his team who believed in the manuscript enough to take it through the publishing process. Thanks also to Taffy Davies for his excellent illustrations that appear throughout this book. Without his artistic skills, neither this book nor www.coffeechats.org would have the "creative draw" they have. Thanks also to my son Luther for the cover design. A big shout out to Paul Manwaring for writing the Foreword and Mark Jarvis whose coaching skills helped to sharpen the Group Discussions and Personal Applications at the end of each chapter.

FOREWORD

This book is rich, a tapestry, a mosaic, and a work of art, history and prophecy all wrapped up in one. Chris has transformed the timeless Sermon on the Mount into a handbook for today. And today, of course, is not just any day but a moment of need, opportunity and challenge.

If all I had initially been told was that this book is an unpacking of the Sermon on the Mount, I might have been a little reluctant, not because I don't hold this Bible passage in high regard, but because most of the books for which I'm asked to write a foreword are biographical, or deal with one strong theme. I am not so sure that I would have considered myself qualified to encourage readers to dive into this classic Bible passage. However, once I started reading, I felt a resounding yes, not because I considered myself capable of sharing the depth of insight which Chris has brought, but because he has woven together so many elements that are dear to my heart and ministry.

Perhaps it is only me, but sermons on these eight beatitudes have often left me feeling uninspired. Even the title of Jesus's great message – the Sermon on the Mount – makes it sound a little too sedentary. But as I read through this beautiful manuscript, that impression was dismantled. In fact, I was immediately intrigued; I felt invited to share a complimentary journey, to climb up the hill (to use Chris's metaphor) that represents the Christian life. Its application is for today and at the same time it presents us with a passionate vision and hope for tomorrow.

When Chris's book arrived, I had recently re-read the beatitudes myself in a variety of translations. It was wonderful to study them again with reference to Richard Wurmbrand

(1909-2001) – a very close friend of my wife's family and a hero for us all, a man whose life beautifully illustrated these kingdom principles. Richard showed us how to live the Christian life under great persecution and trial. Chris cites many other similar heroes to inspire our climb "up the hill". Chris is a great wordsmith. Combining supernatural revelation with natural understanding, he shines fresh light on the glorious yet ancient Word of God, the Bible. He provides a definition of each beatitude at the start of each chapter and this alone is worth studying before delving into what follows. My favourite is Chris's definition for "Blessed are they that Mourn": "A readiness to be broken with what breaks God's heart and a willingness to co-labour with heaven to restore what has been lost on the earth."

This idea of brokenness is both beautiful and encouraging, making the most doubtful and self-critical reader believe that they too were born to climb the same hill. Chris does this kind of thing many times throughout the book, empowering the disempowered, encouraging the discouraged, lighting lamps in the darkness and providing destinations that captivate our hearts and minds. Chris has truly put fresh life into the Sermon on the Mount, as the following paragraph shows:

"To hear this symphony, you need to be prepared to climb. *Life on the Hill* is a study of what Jesus taught His climbing companions (Matthew 5:1-2) – lessons imperative to authentic Christian living in God's alternative society – the Kingdom of Heaven on the earth. Climbers are a strange breed. The desire to climb is only surpassed by a passion to reach the top. Here they may pause to appreciate life on a different level, before commencing their descent."

Chris's ability to evoke hunger, harness desperation, envision the adventurer, and birth the world-changer is evident throughout this book. It is great for the individual reader, ideal for small groups, and it has the quality of genius. It contains revival history, revival passion and desperation, a revival-based perspective on the Word of God (especially the words of Jesus). It redefines what the normal Christian life looks like and calls us onwards and upwards. It is practical as well as inspired, deep enough to make us re-examine ourselves and at the same time encouraging enough for us to believe that we can all play our part. Chris describes what a true expression of the Kingdom looks like and provides great tools for making that a reality in our daily lives.

Above all, this is a book that is good for your heart. In Chris's words: "The heart is the centre or seat of a person's moral decisions, the fulcrum of all feelings, the core of one's character." In the end, I am left with my heart challenged. I feel drawn back into the Word of God and thrust into the glorious future potential for all of us, and especially the Church.

For most of us, the current troubles caused by a worldwide pandemic do not come close to the persecution that Richard Wurmbrand experienced, but we would still do well to underscore one of the final truths which Chris wrote: "In times of trouble, we need to remember that persecution can accomplish in us things that blessing never could."

Chris invites you to read, climb higher, see more, believe for more.

When you have started climbing the hill, allow your hunger and desperation to draw other climbers to join you on a journey into true Kingdom Revival.

This is a book for our times.

It will accomplish great things in you.

Paul Manwaring
Member Senior Leadership Team, Bethel Church, California
Author of: *What on Earth is Glory*, *Kisses from a Good God* and *Things Fathers Do*

CONTENTS

1

A TIME TO CLIMB

"Let your heart soar as high as it will.
Refuse to be average"
A.W. Tozer[1]

The flight director of the ill-fated Apollo 13 mission was a man called Gene Kranz. In the movie *Apollo 13*, he was played by Ed Harris. Kranz is remembered for a remark he made at a critical moment in the mission – a remark that would give motivational impetus to American space exploration. Exemplifying the can-do attitude of Houston's Mission Control, he said, "With all due respect, sir, I believe this is going to be our finest hour."

The context for this, of course, was an explosion in space, after which NASA was faced with the seemingly impossible task of bringing a crippled spacecraft back to earth. With a fifty per cent loss of oxygen and power, some 180,000 nautical miles from earth, Apollo 13 was in trouble. Houston had to find a way to retrieve the three American astronauts lost in space. They had no simulation data to cover this eventuality.

Six minutes after the television coverage of one phase of the journey had finished, Jack Swigert was asked to activate the stirring fans in the oxygen tanks. No one realized that this routine procedure would set off a sequence of near fatal events. Having triggered the "bomb", Commander Jim Lovell messaged those now famous words, "Uh Houston, we've had a problem here!" Thereafter, the staff of Mission Control were

---

1. A.W. Tozer, *The Root of the Righteous* (1955, www.hsraadio.net), page 30, 31.

the only ones to watch the crew of Apollo 13 giving what turned out to be an outstanding professional performance inside the command and lunar module.

What had happened? A mechanical malfunction had triggered a series of incidents causing an explosion which then ruptured an oxygen tank. This in turn resulted in the spacecraft losing breathable air and power at an alarming rate.

Unless Mission Control could find a way to get them back, Jim Lovell, Jack Swigert and Fred Hayes would become the first American astronauts to be lost in space.

Two NASA directors discussed the grim prospects for these three men. They were perceived to have little chance.

"I know what the problems are, Henry," one of them said.

"This could be the worst disaster NASA has ever experienced," the other added.

On hearing this, flight director Gene Kranz spoke the Churchillian words that would set the scene for one of history's greatest achievements.

"With all due respect, sir, I believe this is going to be our finest hour."

Everyone in the room faced the same crisis, but while some saw the probability of a catastrophic loss of life, one man perceived it as an unprecedented opportunity. The difference was all a matter of perspective.

Our Finest Hour

In the Spring of 1940, when Norway, Poland, the Netherlands, Denmark, Belgium and France had been occupied by German troops, Britain stood on the edge of an abyss. The Wehrmacht had raised the swastika over Paris and it only seemed a matter of time before Nazi jackboots would be marching down Whitehall. Britain was gripped by fear. Stopping Hitler's advancing army seemed a lost cause. This was Britain's darkest hour.

On the 125th anniversary of the Battle of Waterloo, Winston Churchill stood to address the House of Commons. Delivering one of the greatest rallying cries in British history, Churchill concluded his thirty-six-minute speech with these prophetic words: "Let us therefore brace ourselves to our duties and so bear ourselves that, if the British Empire and its Commonwealth last for a thousand years, men will still say, 'this was their finest hour.'"[2]

As I sit looking out of my study window on the green and tranquil scenery that surrounds our English cottage, it is hard to believe today that the world is facing a viral pandemic, a health crisis of apocalyptic proportions. With people self-isolating, planes grounded, pubs, schools, restaurants and businesses closed, the world is facing a crisis of unprecedented proportions. Thousands die daily of poverty across the world, but this disease – Covid-19 – is no respecter of persons.

Life seems surreal, as if we have become part of a movie. Any moment, we hope the director will shout, "Cut," and we will walk off the set and return to normality.

At the time of writing, the British government has asked that citizens should "stay at home". Although the current Prime Minister makes comparisons with World War II, it is clear that we face a very different enemy from the one our parents and

---

2. Winstonchurchill.org/resources/speeches/1940-the-finest-hour/their-finest-hour/

grandparents faced. This enemy is invisible; it threatens to take tens of thousands of lives in the UK alone. In this frightening scenario, people are beginning to contemplate their own mortality as doctors are forced to make life-and-death choices. Elderly people are being forced to have traumatic conversations with their children about their final wishes. Truly, our world has been rocked forever by this unseen foe called Covid-19. A few months ago, few had heard of it, but now everything has changed. Terrified of the unseen, people have been panic-buying, stocking up on essential supplies as if someone has pressed the reset button on the Y2K bug. While some are only interested in helping themselves, others are stepping up to join a vast army of volunteers, supporting heroic health workers on the front line. Whatever the coming months and years hold for the world is unclear, but for those who survive this pandemic, life will never be the same again.

Sent to Our Room?

Those of us who lived through the Cuban missile crisis in 1962, the assassination of John F. Kennedy in 1963, the first lunar landing in 1969, and the Twin Towers attack in 2001, remember exactly where we were and what we were doing when the news broke. 2020 will prove to be similar. With the Australian bushfires raging, with East Africa and parts of Asia overrun with billions of swarming locusts, and now with a planetary pandemic, 2020 will be indelibly etched on the minds of those who survive it.

What is this all about? Is God behind all these tragedies, causing immense global suffering? People who study theology distinguish between the decretive and the permissive will of God. The decretive will is what God decrees. If Covid-19 was part of His decretive will, then this would mean God has caused this virus to afflict the earth as a punishment of some kind. The permissive will of God is what He permits. In this scenario, God has not caused and decreed this pandemic. Rather, He is allowing it.

The central revelation of Jesus Christ in the New Testament is that God is the most adoring and affectionate of fathers, slow to anger and abounding in love. To say that God has decreed and caused this pandemic is, frankly, completely in contradiction to this revelation. Only those with a very distorted God-image would claim this. However, it is perfectly reasonable to say that it is an example of the Father's permissive will. Even though it pains His compassionate heart, He is allowing this pandemic so that we will learn to reach out to Him in desperation, with a deep spiritual hunger for His presence.

Although not the author and perpetuator of these things, I therefore wonder if a loving heavenly Father is permitting this crisis to do what earthly fathers sometimes do – send us to our rooms to rethink our behaviour, to reset our moral compasses. Many would say that contemporary Christianity, especially in the West, has become far too comfortable.

Has Christianity become so blasé that it takes a killer virus to get our attention?

Is our perspective of life so skewed that we need to come face to face with our mortality before we make the necessary adjustments to God's will and His ways?

While naturally we might talk in terms of a crisis, spiritually we perhaps need to see this present situation as a crucible. God's gold is in the fire and He has a vested interest in His investment. While politicians and people alike understandably look for a practical and scientifically guided way out, what Christians should be praying for is the way through. Maybe heaven wants to purify and prepare the church for what is about to happen. To live our immediate in the light of an ultimate, we need to adjust and, if necessary, alter our angle of approach to life.

Finding Our Voice

Life on the Hill is a guidebook for those tired of mediocrity. It is for Christ followers who want to live their lives on a different level. Christianity today needs to find its voice. Rather than hearing echoes from some bygone era, the world needs a prophetic voice that points to a better future. Self-isolating Italians took to their balconies to form an impromptu communal choir. They have found their voices. Meanwhile, reserved English people every Thursday at 8pm stood on their doorsteps to applaud and cheer the heroic efforts of the health service. They have found their voice. Now it's time for the voice of Christianity to be heard as well. In God's economy, it is midnight. Like Paul and Silas in jail (Acts 16:16-40), it is time to sing from our place of confinement.

It's time for Christianity to break out of its self-imposed incarceration to declare the goodness of God to the world in which we live.

For too long, a Cinderella culture has paralysed the Christian church, allowing the ugly sisters of intimidation and fear to exile us to the basement of world events. We have allowed others to taunt us and stop us living in our inheritance. It's time to break free of basement thinking and start to enjoy high-level living as sons and daughters of the King. It's time to escape our ghetto mentality and step out onto our balconies and sing the songs of God's grace. It's time to applaud the goodness of God in our lives, so that the Good News reverberates around our neighbourhood. It's time for the earth to hear heavenly anthems with lyrics that speak of a loving heavenly Father waiting with open arms to receive back His prodigal sons and daughters.

When God Calls Time!

The ancient Greeks had two words for time, *chronos* and *kairos*. Whereas *chronos* is more about quantity, *kairos* is about quality. *Chronos* is clock or calendar time. *Kairos* denotes a special moment in time. Guy Chevreau illustrates the difference when he suggests that a pregnant mother is attuned to *kairos* time, to that special moment of delivery, whereas her husband is usually more focused on *chronos* time. Guy writes: "About nine months or so into a pregnancy – *chronos* time – many soon-to-be-mothers shake their husbands by the shoulder and say, 'It's time!' He opens a bleary eye, looks at the clock, and says, 'It's 3:17 in the morning; go back to sleep!' She's on *kairos* time, but he's talking *chronos*. So, he gets shaken again: 'It's time!' and this time he gets it! IT'S TIME!!!"[3]

When God calls *kairos* time, He who exists outside this time/space continuum is talking about something conceived in His own heart that is about to be birthed. This happens when He alone sees fit. For example, when Jesus was born on the earth two thousand years ago, this could be said to have been an event in the chronological time of the world's history. It was something that happened in our *chronos*. At the same time (if you'll pardon the pun), this event was a once-in-a-lifetime – actually, once-in-the-course-of-history – moment in which

---

3. Guy Chevreau, *Catch the Fire: The Toronto Blessing* (New York, NY: HarperCollins, 1995), p. 49.

God did something unique, extraordinary, monumental and, well, history-making. Into our *chronos*, God did something that looked more like *kairos*. Everything had been building up to this *kairos* moment during the *chronos* of history. As a result, Jesus began His ministry by announcing that "the time (*kairos*) is fulfilled" (Mark 1:15, KJV).

As 2020 proceeds, could this be a *kairos* moment in which God is about to birth a second reformation? Are we about to experience the re-emergence of a radical church? Is this the time when heaven's rain will fall on earth's dry ground? Is this the moment the Church breaks free of a building mindset and becomes the true *ecclesia* that God originally intended? Could this be our finest hour?

Climbing and Shining

It is time for Christianity to climb, to break free of earth's gravitational pull and soar to a new level of intimacy with God.

It is time for Christianity to stop living in the shadows of past experiences and to start living in the full assurance of who we are in Christ.

Maybe this is a *kairos* moment in which, rather than acting like stateless misfits, Christians will begin to behave like the legal residents of a city set on a hill, becoming a light that cannot be hidden (Matthew 5:14). It's therefore time to climb. And it's time to shine, to become a beacon of hope to the world, to illuminate the darkness that covers the earth, to bring light to areas of social injustice, poverty and conflict (Isaiah 60:1-3).

No one knows what the coming months will hold but one thing is certain: life will never be the same again. As

Christians, we need to recognize this as a *kairos* moment, bid farewell to a casual and consumerist Christianity and usher in a Church that truly represents the Kingdom of Heaven on earth. The Church cannot continue to function like a gargantuan spiritual machine sustained by weary volunteers. The political systems of hierarchy that have created an out-of-control spiritual monster have to die. This liberal leviathan we call Church, more akin to the entertainment industry than a body of believers doing life together, now needs to stop. The numbers game by which we measure spiritual success needs to cease. The charismatic style of leadership – one that becomes a liability to recover from rather than a goal to aim for – needs to end. The theatrical obsession with how things look must play itself out. It's time to stop moving the deckchairs around the *Titanic*. It's time for the true Church to climb to new heights.

Instead of being Temple-centric (the megachurch), this is the moment when the true biblical *ecclesia* emerges. Every generation has moments that define it. This could be our *kairos* time. 2020 could be remembered in the future as the moment when a brave new Church emerged and true Christianity with it. Now is therefore a good moment to listen again to the opening statements of the Sermon on the Mount in the fifth chapter of Matthew's gospel. As someone has rightly remarked,

---

"If you read the history of the church, you will find it has always been when men and women have taken this sermon seriously, and faced themselves in the light of it, that true revival had come."[4]

---

4. Martyn Lloyd-Jones, *Studies in the Sermon on the Mount* (IVP, 1971).

When we start to live by Jesus's eight Be-Attitudes, we start to soar to new heights.

Little Time

By dedicating this book to the memory of a godly mother, I honour the fact that she not only taught me how to live my life in the pursuit of God, but how to value that most precious of commodities – time. The marginal note in her tatty King James Bible simply read, "Little Time." This was more than a cryptic answer to the question, "What is your life? For you are a mist that appears for a little time and then vanishes" (James 4:14, ESV). This was a commentary on those short fifty-seven years she lived with a sense of divine urgency.

Time is precious, so rather than settle for the lowlands of passivity, let's grab our gear and follow in the footsteps of a master mountaineer called Jesus.

As a roadmap for the life God intended, *Life on the Hill* takes us from the basecamp of total surrender to the summit of godly satisfaction. From this vantage point of godly contentment, we become a people poised to reach out in authentic ways to those living within our sphere of influence.

What if God is shaking the shakeable to establish the unshakeable (Hebrews 12:27)? What if heaven is preparing earth for a spiritual tsunami? What if Christ is calling His Church to leave the plains of casual Christianity, to resist the temptation to remain in the foothills of past experiences, and head for higher ground? What if this is a moment in time to take Jesus's most famous sermon seriously? Because maybe, just maybe, it's time for

- The sons of God to rise up.
- The servants of the Lord to speak up.
- The soldiers of the King to step up.
- And the stewards of grace to wake up.

GROUP DISCUSSION AND PERSONAL APPLICATION GUIDE

Group Discussion:

- Have there been moments of great difficulty in your life which turned out to be moments of great opportunity?
- When, as a Christ-centred community, has the Church been at its best for you?
- Why do you think some of us are so fearful about sharing our faith and how did we end up here?

Personal Application:

- Looking back at the story of your life so far, have there been any kairos moments you can think of in which God gave you a once-in-a-lifetime opportunity to do something significant for Him? If so how did you respond?
- Are you fearful above sharing your faith? If so why?
- If fear is linked with trust, who is it you do not trust, ourselves, others or God?
- Is it time to go to a new level of kingdom vitality, to embrace the Be-Attitudes and to start living *Life on the Hill*?

When it comes to Personal Application we would encourage you to involve a "Spiritual Summiteer" (see page 37) so as to give yourself some level of accountability and guide you on your ongoing journey.

2

THERE'S A MALLORY IN ALL OF US!

*"The greatest danger in life is
not taking the adventure."*

George Mallory[5]

I was a newcomer to book signings, but as soon as I heard his booming voice echoing throughout the store, as soon as I sensed his eccentric personality dominating the room like some monarch holding court, I knew I was in the right place. Bloomsbury publishers had organized regional events for a British icon to sell signed copies of his latest book. When I arrived, his tall, bearded frame seemed to occupy every metre of space in the small inner-city bookstore. I was in the presence of a TV personality and I knew it. Here was an easily recognizable public figure. This middle-aged man had for years been an integral part of British television.

Now I was in the presence of an actor turned mountaineer, a mountaineer turned author. And I was paying homage, like everyone else.

As the queue slowly shortened, I kept catching a glimpse of the unmistakable outline of this gentle giant. Here was a man ten years my senior who at the age of fifty-three had realized

---

5. Words penned by Brian Blessed in the book *The Turquoise Mountain* (Bloomsbury, 1991).

a lifetime's ambition of following in the footsteps of his hero, George Leigh Mallory, who in 1924, with Andrew Irvine, mysteriously disappeared near the summit of Everest. Now signing copies of his latest book, *The Turquoise Mountain* – a detailed account of his journey in the footsteps of his boyhood hero – the legendary figure of Brian Blessed was signing copies in the bookshop.[6]

Mountain Men

The final hours of George Leigh Mallory are cloaked in mystery. On 8th June 1924, Mallory, along with his faithful companion Andrew "Sandy" Irvine, made a final and fateful attempt at achieving the summit of the mountaineers' Holy Grail – Everest. That was the last anyone at the time heard of them. It would take rescuers 75 years to finally discover Mallory's mummified body on the slopes of the summit of Everest, but it was unclear whether Mallory had died on the way up or the way down. The majority of accidents happen on the descent. When the searchers discovered his body – clearly identified by nametags inside his 1920s mountaineering gear – this did little to answer the age-old question, "Did Mallory achieve his lifelong ambition of reaching the summit?"

George Leigh Mallory was every bit your egocentric mountain man. Climbing was in his blood. After being banished from a nursery class as an unruly seven-year-old, Mallory was discovered climbing the roof of Mobberley parish church! It was perhaps no surprise then that, ten days short of his thirty-eighth birthday, Mallory would make an attempt at reaching the summit of the world's highest mountain.

At 12.50 p.m. on the afternoon of 8th June 1924, Noel Odell, who was climbing solo in support of Irvine and Mallory, spoke

---

6. Taken from the back-cover blurb of Brian Blessed, *The Turquoise Mountain* (Bloomsbury, 1991).

of how he saw the clouds briefly part, giving him a glimpse of the two fading figures outlined against the summer sky far above him. Moving expeditiously over the steep rocks with the summit only a thousand feet above them they were, in Odell's words, "last seen heading for the top". Those six words not only form an epitaph for the two climbing superstars; they also form a tribute to the person to whom this book is dedicated, as you'll see.

Described as the Chris Bonington of his day, George Mallory was – for the man signing books in the city of Leicester – the person whose footsteps he longed to follow. Wearing clothing identical to what Mallory wore in 1925, Brain Blessed's dream had been to see how far he could climb in pursuit of his boyhood hero.

Having now made my way to the front of the long and meandering queue, I stood in front of a larger-than-life figure who looked every bit the modern-day version of a mountain man.

With the introductory niceties out of the way, our conversation soon centred on the reason for my interest in both the book and its author.

A little nervous, I wondered how our meeting would go. However, Blessed's winsome smile and cheery voice immediately put me at my ease. Having introduced myself with a customary handshake, the conversation soon turned to the author's inspiration for writing *The Turquoise Mountain* – that is, George Leigh Mallory.

"I'm interested in Mallory," I said, "because I'm interested in the importance and implications of mental attitudes." Then, reusing a chat-up line that had got me into the flight deck of a British Airways passenger jet, I sheepishly added, "I'm researching the importance of a positive mental attitude on people's behaviour." I lacked the courage to share the whole truth, that I was looking at the teachings of the biblical Jesus from the Sermon on the Mount to write a book on the subject.

This introductory remark had worked well on the approach to Belfast International Airport. It resulted in me securing the third seat on the flight deck. The pilot asked me to remain silent as I observed the inner workings of a flight crew on the landing path. Once we had taxied to our gate, however, the Captain allowed me to engage in a conversation about the importance of an aircraft's angle of approach.

More of that later!

I am happy to say that the same line worked well with Brian Blessed! My remark caused him to talk eloquently about his lifetime fascination with the exploits of George Mallory. He concluded by passing on the following story.

"As Mallory was about to leave his family for his ill-fated climb, the gathered journalists asked him if, in the light of being a family man, climbing Everest wasn't dangerous. Mallory replied, 'Yes, it is dangerous, but the greatest danger in life is to miss the adventure.'"

Then, opening my copy of *The Turquoise Mountain*, Brian Blessed penned these words.

Lots of Love to Chris and Tina,
Brian Blessed.
Mallory said, "Yes, it is dangerous going to Mount Everest.
But the greatest danger in life, is not taking the adventure."

Biblical Mountain Men

Although I admire Mallory, he is not the first mountain man I've read about; the Bible is full of them. In fact, we can easily forget that some of the greatest personal revelations were given by God on the top of mountains!

Noah experienced God's saving grace on Mount Ararat.

Abraham found God's substitutional provision on Mount Moriah.

Elijah demonstrated the purpose and power of God on Mount Carmel.

Moses discovered the tangible presence of a holy God on top of Mount Sinai.

Maybe the Russian mountaineer Anatoli Boukreev has a point when he says, "Mountains are not stadiums where I satisfy my ambition to achieve; they are the cathedrals where I practice my religion."[7]

Whether it's for the personal challenge, gaining a greater perspective, enjoying a different atmosphere, or simply being alone with our thoughts, mountains feature prominently in God's purposes. The example of these heroic biblical climbers calls forth in us a desire to go to the next level, to leave the nursery slopes of spiritual immaturity, turn our back on the plains of passivity, and become fully committed to attaining the summit of God's purposes. As A.W. Tozer writes,

"Vital Christianity implies the element of hazard, of speculation, of splendid gamble . . . when there's no risk the so-called venture is dead – God works as long as his people live daringly."[8]

To quote Mallory, yes, it's risky, but the greatest danger in life is to miss the adventure.

---

7. At the site of Annapurna base-camp there is a memorial to Boukreev which includes a quotation of his: "Mountains are not stadiums where I satisfy my ambition to achieve, they are the cathedrals where I practice my religion." https://www.adventure-journal. com/2016/09/hero-of-everest-tragedy-was-climbing-prodigy/
8. Cited in https://www.hsraadio.net/raamat/Tozer_TheBestOfTozer.pdf.

The Settler Mentality

In a risk-averse society, there is often an inherent lack of desire to lay everything on the line for a greater good. This same lack of adventure permeates the Church.

The lowlands of casual Christianity are overpopulated with a consumerist generation happy to live off the ground attained by their parents and grandparents.

Today, we live in an age of entitlement in which people are happy to settle in the land for which a previous generation gave everything. Many Christians casually eat the honey and drink the milk that others sacrificed so much for us to enjoy. Think of the birth of the house church movement. Thank God for the Moses generation who brought many of us out of the bondage of organized religion. Thank God for the Joshua generation who brought us into the fulness of the Holy Spirit. Be thankful for the past but also have a dream for the future. There is still much land to occupy and those whose ambition is only to be a settler will fail to achieve it.

Preferring to copy rather than create, risk-averse leaders take the safe option. Becoming hesitant to think and act outside the box, short-sighted leaders recreate in others a settler mentality that falls far short of God's ultimate intent. In every generation, God has always raised up those who live with a big-picture consciousness, people who live and breathe for God's larger purpose. Who will rise to take on that role today? Speaking to the Royal Geographical Society, the explorer extraordinaire David Hempleman-Adams – the man who crossed the North Pole and skied down Everest – addressing the issue of people's unwillingness to take risk concluded, "We are becoming a society of softies. It is a crazy reflection of our times that we are surrounding our children in cotton wool... they will not be able to cope with risk when they encounter it as adults."[9]

While most may not want to be involved in extreme sports, more of us in the Church need to be willing to take godly risks to extend the purposes of heaven on earth. Where are the people like David's mighty men who willingly risked their lives for their king (1 Chronicles 11:19)? Where are the likes of Barnabas and Paul who risked their own necks for the work of God (Acts 15:26)? Where are those like Epaphroditus who risked his life for the cause of Christ (Philippians 2:30)? Where are the people who will leave the plains of passivity, accepting that being a Christ-follower includes "the element of hazard, of speculation, of splendid gamble," and push for a Christianity that exists on a different level altogether?

Spiritual Summiteers

Every mountaineer who attempts Everest knows the importance of climbing with a recommended guide. As natives of the region, Sherpas have grown accustomed to the altitude. Known as "Summiteers", the best Sherpas are those who have helped others to successfully reach the top on multiple occasions.

---

9. Quoted in John Humphrys, *Devil's Advocate* (London: Hutchinson, 1999), p. 15.

Successful mountaineers put their trust in someone who has travelled this way before.

Although the name Dick Iverson will mean little to most of you, he was the spiritual Sherpa who accompanied my first attempt at understanding and living the Sermon on the Mount. A godly man with years of experience, Pastor Iverson taught me the true meaning of what I call *Life on the Hill*. Using terms like "Be-attitudes" or "Attitudes-to-be", Dick Iverson was the first person to explain to me how these kingdom mindsets are designed to show us how to rely completely on God and how to relate authentically to people. He not only pointed the way, he took me and others by the hand, and led us in the ways of kingdom living. Trekking with us through the opening verses of Matthew chapter 5, he showed us how these *be-attitudes* are a place to live, not just a space to visit. When the terrain became difficult, he spoke words of encouragement. When we stumbled, he helped us to our feet again. When we felt like giving up, he urged us to press on.

For those reading *Life on the Hill* with a commitment to complete the climb, I would strongly encourage you to find your own "Irvin" or "Iverson". Look for a spiritual Sherpa who will journey with you, a trusted friend who will ask the hard questions and keep you accountable. As we read in the book of Ecclesiastes 4:9-10, "Two are better than one . . . For if they fall, the one will lift up his fellow" (KJV).

Although latent in some and self-evident in others, we all have an inherent desire to aim higher and find that elusive someone or something that will bring us a deep sense of satisfaction and achievement.

We may not possess a T-type personality that loves extreme sports and risky living, but deep inside the human heart is a desire to find fulfilment, to break free of the mundane and find higher ground.

If Christianity shouts anything to us, it's a refusal to settle for the mundane. In the Bible, Caleb at the age of eighty-five claimed an inheritance promised some forty-five years earlier. Mentored by Moses, he observed a man who seven times climbed Sinai to discover the radiant presence of God, and who then led others in the ways of God. Although an ageing octogenarian, Caleb asked Joshua to give him the hill country. With no desire to settle for the ordinary, Caleb longed to live his concluding years engrossed in the extraordinary. While those half his age preferred to settle, Caleb was a pioneer.

I believe there is a Caleb Spirit in all of us – a "different attitude" (Numbers 14:24) that refuses to settle for the mundane. *Life on the Hill* is a call for those whose epitaph will read, "Last seen heading for the top!"

Although the ascent will be a steep learning curve, the satisfaction drawn from reaching the summit will be immense and the reward will be that we get to equip others to be risk-attuned rather than risk-averse.

Built around the eight *be-attitudes* outlined in Matthew 5:1-11, *Life on the Hill* is a road map for those entering and enjoying a life lived in that advancing and adventurous reality that Jesus called the kingdom of God.[10]

If you are ready, let us begin the ascent to a life lived on a different level!

There is a Mallory in all of us.

GROUP DISCUSSION AND
PERSONAL APPLICATION GUIDE

Group Discussion:

- When it comes to mountaineering, are you the "get-up-and-go" type or the "stick-to-ground-level" kind of person?
- If not a mountain, where do you go to meet with God and how does it change your perspective on things?
- What are your "barriers to entry"[11] when it comes to a time alone with God?

Personal Application:

- Who is your inspirational hero and what is it about them that inspires you?
- What three characteristics would you look for in a "Spiritual Sherpa"?
- Are you ready to name your "Spiritual Summiteer"?

When it comes to Personal Application we would encourage you to involve a "Spiritual Summiteer" (see page 37) so as to give yourself some level of accountability and guide you on your ongoing journey.

---

11. "Barrier to Entry" is a business term used to speak of those people, objects and events that can stop a business going to the next level.

3

SEARCHING FOR GOD KNOWS WHAT

"If you want to build a ship, don't drum up the men to gather wood, divide the work and give orders. Instead, teach them to yearn for the vast and endless sea."

Antoine de Saint (1900–1944)[12]

In the early hours of a warm Californian morning, a bleary-eyed musician woke with music on his mind. Fumbling for his guitar and the portable recorder conveniently positioned on the nightstand, he managed to lay down an eight-note riff and a five-word lyric, before falling back to sleep. The words? "I can't get no satisfaction."

The rest, as they say, is history.

Newspaper headlines would read: "Early-morning recording session brings struggling band global success!"

Although initially regarded as nothing more than an album-filler, this five-fold lyric was destined to become one of the greatest rock-and-roll songs ever recorded. Even in his wildest dreams, the composer could never have envisaged how five simple words would resonate with so many people. Yet, by turning a rough recording into a musical masterpiece, pop legends Keith Richards and Mick Jagger caught the heart of an emerging generation and produced their first American number one hit.

---

12. https://www.la-grange.net/2010/12/29/saint-exupery

Perhaps the true lyrical genius of what this dynamic duo created was not in the fame and fortune this song would inevitably bring, but in the fact that they had inadvertently stumbled on a social anthem that defined a decade.

This was the "Swinging Sixties", an age of social revolution, when people questioned the acceptable norms of music, dress, drugs and formality. Sandwiched between the "Fabulous Fifties" and the "Super Seventies", the Sixties was, to borrow a phrase, "The best of times and the worst of times."

While some would argue that this was a defining moment in human history, others would claim that the Sixties were a turning point when "common decency" became uncommon.

That said, some would advocate that this particular era was no different from any other; people were simply doing what they had always done; that is, search for that something or someone that will truly satisfy the deep desires of the heart.

More than a pop song with possible sexual connotations, "I can't get no satisfaction" seems to reverberate with humanity's discontent. Taking second place in *Rolling Stone* magazine's "500 Greatest Songs of All Time", this iconic composition not only characterizes a period of history, it somehow manages to echo the emptiness of the human heart. Richard's early-morning recording session was perhaps a wakeup call – an eight-note riff that reminds us that true fulfilment is difficult to find.

Trivial Pursuits

Everyone wants to find that elusive something or someone that will make them happy. When we were children, we thought that the latest video game or must-have Christmas present would do it. But it didn't. As teenagers, we believed that the latest fashion item, phone upgrade, good exam results, those sporting achievements, finding that "significant other", would bring contentment. But they all left us wanting more. As adults, we wondered if a better job, bigger house, faster car would bring fulfilment. They did not. It seems that all of us are singing from the U2 song sheet: "Still haven't found what I'm looking for!"

With more than 660 million of the earth's population without adequate sanitation, living on less than £2 a day,[13] the average Westerner has so much in comparison to the rest of the world. But the reality is, we continue to play the game of trivial pursuits believing the more we have, the better we will feel, when the reality is that prosperity and possessions are doing little to bring a lasting satisfaction to the inner longing of the human heart. While the have-nots struggle for survival, and the haves are dissatisfied with what they possess, human beings are locked in an endless cycle of searching for satisfaction, thinking they have found it, only to be disappointed, and then start the whole process again. Like drinking sea water, these things just make us thirstier than we were before. Or as C.S. Lewis writes, 'Human history . . . is the long terrible story of man trying to find something other than God which will make him happy.'[14]

As a thirty-something, Stephen Altrogge writes, "My generation is desperately trying to make sense out of life. They are groping and grasping for meaning, caught in an endless existential cycle that leaves many of them despairing and cynical. They don't have an objective bigger than their own happiness and satisfaction and self-fulfilment . . . they stumble from one thing to the next without having any grand sense of

---

13. See www.globalissues.org/article/26/poverty-facts-and-stats
14. C.S. Lewis, *Mere Christianity* (first published in Great Britain by Geoffrey Bles, 1952).

purpose or direction. We are a generation of wanderers and waifs, of strugglers and stragglers, blown from one thing to the next, always searching but never finding." Altrogge concludes by saying, "God created us in such a way that we can never satisfy ourselves. No matter how much inner exploration, self-worship, or self-fulfilment we experience, we simply cannot satisfy ourselves. Whether we climb to the top of Maslow's hierarchy of needs or the top of the business world, the results are the same."[15] Truly, fulfilment is hard to find.

Like Edison searching for his lightbulb moment, Shackleton endeavouring to find the South Pole, or Stanley looking for his Livingstone, each generation, while marching to a different drumbeat, is humming the same melancholy tune. Whether it is the astronomer searching for new planets through a telescope, or the scientist looking for new cures through a microscope, if our pursuit distracts us from the ultimate source of true contentment, then all our endeavours, no matter how honourable, are fundamentally floored.

The Five A's

Misters Jagger and Richards were perhaps unaware that their eight-note riff was just a restatement of a theme that has been explored for thousands of years. There was nothing particularly original about their refrain. Human beings have expressed this deep ache for satisfaction since time immemorial. As King Solomon once said, there is nothing new under the sun. Indeed, had the Rolling Stones been looking for a celebrity figure to endorse their lyrics, there is perhaps no better person than Solomon, the Old Testament king.

---

15. Stephen Altrogge, *Untamable God* (Copyright © 2013 Stephen Altrogge), pp.10-11.

A wise and wealthy man, this playboy prince spent years searching for that elusive something or someone that would bring him true and lasting contentment.

Solomon's life was full of wasted opportunities. His expensive and somewhat erratic search for happiness had tragic consequences (1 Kings 11:9-13). For a man who seemingly had everything, his life was a sad reflection on the extremes that people will go to in their search for contentment.

Solomon set out on a flawed quest for self-fulfilment. Living a life of excess and extremes, when one avenue failed to achieve the desired effect he would simply change tack and head off in another direction. Zigzagging his way through life, Solomon's unabated desires would side-track him into Amusement, Alcohol, Achievement, Acquisition and Arousal. None of these would provide satisfaction.

Living his immediate with no thought of the ultimate, like so many before and since, Solomon reduced his life to a game of trivial pursuits.

- **Amusement:** at the risk of oversimplifying the life of this complex character, the reality is King Solomon mirrors modernity in our relentless pursuit of contentment. Always searching for that elusive someone or something to fulfil his longing for the elixir of life, when one avenue proved to be a dead-end Solomon chose to search elsewhere. In his quest for amusement, Solomon said, "Let's go for it – experiment with pleasure, have a good time!" Sadly, he concluded that "there was nothing to it, nothing but smoke. What do I think of the fun-filled life? Insane! Inane!" (Ecclesiastes 2:1-3, MSG).

Whether we call it entertainment or escapism, we spend a staggering amount of time consuming all forms of amusement. The average British householder views subscriptions to entertainment packages a close second to paying for housing, fuel, power and transport. To quote Neil Postman's famous book, we are "amusing ourselves to death".[16] We are obsessed with having a laugh, whether it's through listening to cynical stand-up comics, or through watching TV game shows. Tragically, this desperate search for entertainment has even made inroads into Christianity.

> ## To make God more palatable, we risk turning eternal things into just another commodity to consume.

Taking the route of amusement to find lasting satisfaction proves to be a mirage – an illusion that creates disillusionment.

- **Alcohol:** when amusement fails, Solomon turns to alcohol. He sums up the absurdity of this when he writes, "With the help of a bottle of wine and with all the wisdom I could muster, I tried my level best to penetrate the absurdity of life. I wanted to get a handle on anything useful we mortals might do during the years we spend on this earth" (Ecclesiastes 2:3, MSG). With alcohol-related hospital admissions rising year on year at an alarming

---

16. Neil Postman, *Amusing Ourselves to Death* (Methuen, 1985). "When a population becomes distracted by trivia, when cultural life is redefined as a perpetual round of entertainments, when serious public conversation becomes a form of baby-talk, when, in short, a people become an audience, and their public business a vaudeville act, then a nation finds itself at risk; culture-death is a clear possibility." For a useful summary of the context and content of this seminal book, see https://en.wikipedia.org/wiki/Amusing_Ourselves_to_Death.

rate in England, alcohol is still a common resource, a first resort, for satisfaction seekers.[17] Whether it's in a quaint English pub, a quintessentially German beer garden, or in the all-important champagne wedding reception, alcohol is deeply embedded in the European way of life; it is the oldest recreational drug. If amusement doesn't do it for us, then maybe alcohol will. But with 150,000 alcohol-related deaths in the USA each year[18] and 40,000 in the UK,[19] the negatives of a life lived with excess seem to far outweigh the positives.

- **Achievement:** when neither amusement nor alcohol have the desired effects, Solomon falls into the performance trap. With a long list of personal achievements, you would think that Solomon would have found a sense of fulfilment. He could say that he had "built houses, planted vineyards, designed gardens and parks and planted a variety of fruit trees in them, made pools of water to irrigate the groves of trees" (Ecclesiastes 2:4-6, MSG). However, whether he was working as a builder, wine-seller, landscape gardener or civil engineer, nothing seemed to give him fulfilment.

When our personal identity is wrapped up in what we do rather than who we are, we run the risk of suffering from approval addiction.

---

17. There were 1.2 million admissions to NHS hospitals in the UK during 2017–2018, see https://digital.nhs.uk/data-and-information/publications/statistical/statistics-on-alcohol/2019/part-1#:~:text=There%20were%201.2%20million%20estimated,7.2%25%20of%20all%20hospital%20admissions.
18. http://blog.oup.com/2010/01/drugs-2/tx/drugs/survey/
19. www.bbc.co.uk/sn/tvradio/programmes/horizon/broadband/

Fixated with achieving one more goal in order to feel appreciated, approved and accepted by those around us, we can so easily end up feeling dizzy as we spin uncontrollably on a downward spiral of addiction.

- **Acquisitions:** thousands of years before the Western world worshipped at shopping malls designed to look like temples, Solomon wrote, "I bought slaves, male and female, who had children, giving me even more slaves; then I acquired large herds and flocks, larger than any before me in Jerusalem. I piled up silver and gold, loot from kings and kingdoms" (Ecclesiastes 2:7-8, MSG). While today's high streets pamper to a consumerist culture, advertisers make us feel like a lesser person if we do not continually upgrade what we have, be it our phone, car, home or designer cloths. Clever and manipulative branding appeals to this appetite for more. We become slaves to fashion, or digital slaves. What begins as an essential item turns into an idol for which we sacrifice time, energy and finance.

Without realizing it, we have become worshippers at the altar of commodities in the cathedrals of consumerism.

Armed with this knowledge, advertisers preach a "must-have" gospel. Paying homage to the god of commercialism, the faithful attend their weekly session of retail therapy with religious devotion. Solomon had a bank balance that placed him in the ranks of the super-rich, yet he still pokes fun at our tendency to buy yet another lottery ticket, join a get-rich scheme, or hope that one day all our ships will come in loaded with more stuff to satisfy our hunger for contentment. His timeless words are worth meditating on today. "Yet when I reflected on everything . . . I concluded: 'All these achievements and possession are ultimately profitless – like chasing the wind! There is nothing gained from them on the earth'" (Ecclesiastes 2:11, NET).

- **Arousal:** Solomon's search for satisfaction included what many believe was the main theme in the song "I can't get no satisfaction" – sex. Put sex in a sentence and it will probably get a reader's attention. Sadly, what God intended to be a beautiful part of a lifelong commitment between a man and woman has become a sordid affair. Researchers today reckon that the top 23 million searches on Google are to do with sex. Finding some form of sexual stimulus has become the avid pursuit of people looking for satisfaction. In every human heart, God has placed a search engine. The trouble is, most of us would rather turn to Google than to God. King Solomon could have had whatever or whoever he wanted; he stated, "I gathered a chorus of singers to entertain me with song, and – most exquisite of all pleasures – voluptuous maidens for my bed" (Ecclesiastes 2:8, MSG). Solomon boasts, "I had all the women a man could want." With a harem of 700 wives and 300 paid mistresses, he was justified in saying that, but as with all his previous wayward appetites, even the highs of sexual arousal left him feeling empty.

To summarise: although our desires and appetites are God-given, left to their own devices our emotions will take us off track. Once Adam and Eve had taken the forbidden fruit, this inbuilt God-given bias for doing good became a counterbalancing tendency towards doing wrong. Humanity's healthy desires turned into unhealthy habits that in turn morphed into unwholesome addictions. How we need Solomon's wisdom! "[I've] looked most carefully into everything, searched out all that is done on this earth. And let me tell you, there's not much to write home about. God hasn't made it easy for us. I've seen it all and it's nothing but smoke . . . and spitting into the wind" (Ecclesiastes 1:12-14, MSG). Echoing the same thought, Solomon concludes his search for fulfilment by saying, "Smoke, nothing but smoke . . . There's nothing to anything – it's all smoke. What's there to show for a lifetime of work, a lifetime of working your fingers to the bone? . . . Everything's boring, utterly boring – no one can find a meaning in it" (Ecclesiastes 1:2-11, MSG).

True Fulfilment

I once heard an international public speaker repeat a God-given prophetic word he heard as a teenager that said, "If you long for me like I long for you, you will be satisfied." This is not only the conclusion we draw from Solomon's life, but a perfect introduction to the eight Be-Attitudes Jesus taught His disciples on a Galilean hillside two thousand years ago, that the ultimate source of true satisfaction is God.

When we lock ourselves into an endless cycle of searching for God knows what, sooner or later we have to reflect on the words of the Old Testament writer who says, "We work to feed our appetites; meanwhile our souls go hungry" (Ecclesiastes 6:7, MSG). Alison Morgan puts it like this: "In this new world, everything is possible, and most of it is for sale . . . advertisers sell not products but identities, lifestyles and dreams . . . We buy leisure . . . we buy relationships . . . we buy bodies . . . we buy experiences." She concludes, "The postmodern world invites us to slake our thirst by drinking deeply from the golden goblet of consumerism. We drink, only to find that we are drinking salt water."[20]

Lost in a mist of our own making, mankind is fumbling through life searching for the source of true fulfilment.

Trying everything legal and sometimes illegal, no stone is left unturned to find that satisfaction. Pop icons, megastars and other public figures make headlines in their pursuit of pleasure. Either unable or unwilling to control their appetites, they throw off inhibitions, break down barriers and step into unfamiliar territory, trying anything to experience another high of happiness. Blurring the edges of what is seen as acceptable behaviour, nothing is off limits in their bid to find fulfilment.

The ancient Hebrew prophets, who believed we could waste our lives in the pursuit of things that could never truly satisfy, asked this question: "Why do you spend your money on junk food, your hard-earned cash on cotton candy?" Seeing our daily pursuit as pointless, the prophet's advice is this: "Listen to me, listen well: Eat only the best, fill yourself with only the finest. Pay attention, come close now, listen carefully to my life-giving, life-nourishing words" (Isaiah 55:1-5, MSG). In saying this, the prophet was not publishing some new diet. He wasn't some fitness freak advertising a fat-busting formula. He was encouraging his listeners to feed on the Scriptures. Thousands of years later, a Rabbi from Nazareth would join in this same symphony by repeating these words: "Man does not live by bread alone, but man lives by every word that proceeds out of the mouth of the LORD" (Deuteronomy 8:3, AMP).

---

20. Alison Morgan, *The Wild Gospel: Bringing Truth to Life* (Monarch, 2004), pp. 171–172.

Back to the Future

Robert Coles, now in his late eighties, was once described by *Time* magazine as, "The most influential living psychiatrist in the US." Coles' five-volume series *Children of Crisis* ran to more than a million words, earning him a Pulitzer Prize. Later selected for the MacArthur Foundation's Genius Award, Coles spent twenty-five years researching the effects of poverty and wealth on children.

In a moving account of Cole's conversion to Christianity, Philip Yancey tells how an interview with a disadvantaged, uneducated, six-year-old New Orleans slum dweller revolutionized his life. Yancey writes this:

> "By the time the last of the *Children in Crisis* volumes had been published, Robert Coles had ended up not in a new place, but in a very old place. He had travelled thousands of miles, recorded miles of tape and written a million words, all of which pointed right back to the Sermon on the Mount. He had discovered that the poor are mysteriously blessed and that the rich live in peril. He had learned that what matters most comes not from without – the circumstances of life – but from within, inside the heart of an individual man or woman."[21]

Coles himself concluded, "Nothing I discovered about the makeup of human beings contradicts in any way what I learn from the Hebrew prophets, and from Jesus and the lives of those he touched. Anything I can say as a result of my research into human behaviour is a mere footnote to those lives in the Old and New Testaments."

What if "searching for God knows what" is more of a solution than a critique? What if God really does know what

---

21. Philip Yancey, *Christianity Today magazine* (February 1987).

we should be searching for? What if this idiom, far from being a sardonic and melancholy cry, is a declaration of truth? I may not be a shopaholic, or addicted to entertainment, but what if my online presence is becoming a major distraction to spiritual things? What if our addictions, which trigger the release of dopamine into our brains, do not give us satisfaction? When laptops, smartphones and iPads keep us connected with others but disconnected from God, we need to ask if they are pathways and portals to true contentment. What if our virtual connections are causing a spiritual disconnect?

And here's the big question.

What if the source of true satisfaction is rooted in an intimate relationship with Father God?

Like Coles, so many of us search throughout the world only to find ourselves right back where we started, hearing the cry of a loving heavenly Father calling out for holy communion with us. Our search for long-term satisfaction is not dependent on the external stimuli of Acquisitions, Achievements, Amusement, Alcohol or Arousal. They are found in the teachings of Jesus!

What if the Sermon on the Mount, given by the Rabbi from Nazareth two thousand years ago, is the roadmap to true satisfaction?

What if this most famous sermon in history shows us where we can find a life of fulfilment and deep contentment?

GROUP DISCUSSION AND PERSONAL APPLICATION GUIDE

Group Discussion:

- What in your teenage years did you pursue to find fulfilment?'

- Do you think any of Solomon's trivial pursuits resonate with 21st-century life?

- Would you agree with the statement that, "Entertainment has even made inroads into Christianity?" If so how and why?

- Did the pandemic of 2020 change your perspective?

Personal Application:

- To stop a life of trivial pursuits will require us admitting the problem before changing direction. Such life-changing actions should never be attempted alone. Talk to your "Spiritual Summiteer" about those issues that have become a diversion in your life?

When it comes to Personal Application we would encourage you to involve a "Spiritual Summiteer" (see page 37) so as to give yourself some level of accountability and guide you on your ongoing journey.

4

LIFE ON THE HILL

"Everything can be taken from a man but one thing: the last of the human freedoms – to choose one's attitude in any given set of circumstance, to choose one's own way."
Victor E. Frankl[22]

The influential Irish playwright George Bernard Shaw is credited with saying that "Britain and America are two nations divided by a common language." As an Englishman who once lived in the United States, I can categorically state that Mr Shaw was right; words carry a variety of meanings for different people in different contexts. Some of my best preaching humour has often been lost in translation in America!

A friend and church leader discovered the truth of Shaw's observation the hard way. Having come from an English boarding school background, and a career as a high-ranking Army officer, Stephen [not his real name] could be regarded as the stereotypical Englishman through and through. While serving as a church leader in downtown Chicago, he quickly came to learn how differently Americans understood his English. Having finished his Sunday-morning sermon, he proceeded to dismiss the congregation with the following statement: "Well, it's been a great morning but I'm sure you're all ready for lunch. So, let's go home and enjoy a great Sunday joint." He was, of course, referring to the English Sunday tradition of roast beef. Unfortunately, for downtown Chicagoans, enjoying a joint had other connotations altogether!

---

22. Victor E. Frankl, *Man's Search for Meaning* (Rider, 2004), p. 75.

Changing Locations

If you emigrate to the USA, you cannot ignore the fact that you are living in a different location and time zone, surrounded by people who speak the same language in different ways. To fully enter and enjoy this new environment, you will need to change your way of life. To ignore a different time zone and insist on living as you had before will cause all kinds of difficulties both to yourself and those in your sphere of influence.

When a person decides to follow Jesus, their new home is called the Kingdom of Heaven. This is the new reality that we are called to indwell. We learn to live according to a different culture – the culture of heaven. In doing this, we need to learn to embrace heaven's values and we need to start to speak in the language, the vocabulary, of this new and otherworldly kingdom. Failing to adapt to this new context, failing to embrace this new language, will lead to disaster. Our task is to make the necessary alterations in what we believe and in the ways we behave.

So, then, what does this heavenly culture look like?

When Jesus began His ministry on earth two thousand years ago, He described the alternative society that He expected His followers to create and He gave us new language to describe this heavenly community. This vision is as vital and relevant today as it was then.

The truth is, Christians have, by a work of divine grace, emigrated to a different reality that demands an alternative lifestyle.

As residents of the Kingdom of Heaven, we are called to do life differently. When the apostle Paul described this spiritual transformation and relocation, he wrote these words (Colossians 1:13-14, MSG):

"God rescued us from dead-end alleys and dark dungeons. He's set us up in the kingdom of the Son he loves so much, the Son who got us out of the pit we were in, got rid of the sins we were doomed to keep repeating."

Through a process of spiritual rebirth, we have translocated from an oppressive regime to life under the government of a loving heavenly Father. Just as any incoming government worth its salt will want to introduce social, fiscal, moral and political reforms, so the government of heaven creates a new vision, new values and a whole new vocabulary. The difference between political systems and heaven's kingdom is this: political powers can only restrain the lawless heart through legislation. The Kingdom of Heaven has the power to *change* the human heart through regeneration. Indeed, the Kingdom of Heaven is the *only* reality that can do this, which is why it is the hope for our world. Only when we think differently will we act differently.

To change the way we think so that we in turn change the way we behave is high on God's agenda.

The Sermon on the Mount in Matthew 5 – 7 is so called because of the geographical location where Jesus delivered His most famous address. In this history-making sermon, He presented a timeless picture of the character and conduct of those living in God's alternative society which is why it is sometimes referred to as "the Manifesto of the Kingdom". When Jesus delivered this message, it sent shockwaves through the corridors of religious power. It is still doing so today.

Life on the Hill looks at the eight opening statements of this sermon. Although these eight statements are traditionally referred to as "the beatitudes", I prefer to use phrases like "Be-Attitudes" and "Attitudes-to-be", or, as we are about to see below, "An Angle of Approach to Life".

Life on the Hill

Just as the Ten Commandments can be divided into two groups of sayings, the same is true of the Be-Attitudes. The first four attitudes are attitudes of ascent; they teach us how to *rely* on God. They describe what a spiritual life at high altitude looks like. The second four are attitudes of descent; they teach us how to *relate* to people, especially when the context is one of hostility from those powers that war against God's alternative society. They describe what life down in the valleys looks like.

LIFE ON THE HILL
LIVING AT DIFFERENT LEVELS

'It's time to CLIMB'

'It's time to SHINE'

A1 - RICH MAN, POOR MAN

A2 - GOOD GRIEF

A3 - DON'T BUCK AUTHORITY

A4 - LAST SEEN HEADING FOR THE TOP

A5 - STRANGER ON A TRAIN

A6 - MOTIVES MATTER

A8 - THERE MAY BE TROUBLE AHEAD

> **For those venturing into this teaching for the first time let me say this: the Sermon on the Mount is no picnic in the park today.**

When these words were first broadcast, it resulted in "the crowds [being] astonished at his teaching" (Matthew 7:28-29, ESV). The word "astonished" literally means "they received a blow".[23] The principles that Jesus presented proved amazing to those who had ears to hear and provided a knockout blow to formal religion.

Jesus described a new code of practice, a different way of doing life, for those living in the Kingdom of Heaven on earth. Becoming a Christ follower therefore does not mean a spiritual tweaking of our behaviour, a tinkering with our weekend routine, but a fundamental change of beliefs resulting in a change in our behaviour. Jesus did not come to adjust our religious practices but to transform the human condition.

In short, the Be-Attitudes describe what life on the hill looks like.

Attitude and Altitude

Frequent fliers will at some point in their lives have heard the following announcement: "Good morning. This is your captain speaking. We have just received final clearance from air traffic control and are about to begin our approach to London Heathrow. We trust you have enjoyed your flight and apologize for any delays."

As the aircraft begins to descend, passengers become aware of familiar landmarks as the plane breaks through the clouds.

---

23. *Thayer's Greek-English Lexicon of the New Testament* (Baker Book House, 1986).

The River Thames shimmers in the morning sun as it snakes its way through the busy metropolis and on to the North Sea. Big Ben and the Houses of Parliament nestle neatly beside the river. The Tower of London and Tower Bridge are both clearly visible in the half light of a grey November morning.

Now into the closing stages of a well-rehearsed routine, the flight crew busy themselves with the details that precede every landing. Some remove what remains of an inflight meal. Others make their way up and down the sloping aisles checking that each passenger has fastened their seatbelt.

As the angle of descent becomes more acute, the pilot begins to turn the aircraft towards the runway. Passengers wait with a mixture of excitement and anxiety for the now imminent landing. The clearly defined lights of the approach path mark the way ahead as the plane's descent becomes more pronounced.

As all this goes on, the relative calm of the cabin stands in stark contrast to the hive of activity on the flight deck. While the aircraft maintains its flight pattern, the captain, first officer and flight engineer make numerous decisions as they watch the dials and digital displays that form a maze of instrumentation, all relaying information about the plane's performance. In a matter of minutes, the aircraft will be committed to a course of action that would be difficult to abort. A wrong decision now could mean the difference between life and death. One instrument is critical – the Attitude Direction Indicator (ADI), sometimes called the "Master Instrument". As a result of numerous calculations and minor adjustments – some manual, some computerized – the aircraft is aligned to the runway. The angle of descent and airspeed are checked and rechecked as the aircraft draws towards the runway like metal to a magnet. Central to the pilot's line of vision, the all-important ADI keeps the crew informed and ensures a safe landing.

"What's this got to do with human attitudes?" I hear you asking.

"Everything!"

When I first studied human attitudes, I decided that the dictionary would be a good starting point. As I thumbed through the pages, I found the appropriate section. Attest, attic, attire . . . attitude. I expected to discover a veritable gem of truth when I began to read. The word attitude was defined as "the position of an aircraft". Surely, I was mistaken. I must have inadvertently read the definition for "altitude". I checked and rechecked the reference. No, it was correct; "attitude" was clearly defined as "the position of an aircraft".

Realizing I needed expert help and technical know-how, I decided to call my father-in-law. As a retired Flight Lieutenant in the Royal Air Force, he would be able to shed some light on this subject. Within moments, he had confirmed that the dictionary definition is correct. He proceeded in layman's terms to explain how in every aircraft there are three imaginary lines of axis: one runs from wingtip to wingtip, another from nose to tail and the third runs vertically from the point at which the first two cross. It is on these three imaginary lines that a pilot positions the aircraft. When the plane alters its angle of ascent or descent on any of these three axes, the Attitude Direction Indicator visually records the movement. These changing angles are therefore called the "attitude of the aircraft". Hence the dictionary definition. This all led me to this thought:

Our mental attitude is our angle of approach to people, objects and events in life. Get the attitude wrong, and disaster follows.

That an attitude is our angle of approach to life is the premise on which *Life on the Hill* is based. It is a traceable thread through every chapter. When we choose our attitudes, these choices have a profound impact on our lives and the lives of others.

Imprints and Blueprints

Attitudes are not innate or inborn, neither are they accidental. They are learned reactions, ways of responding that we absorb from parents, teachers, peers and various people who affected our formative years. Our beliefs, and consequently our behaviour, are the result of a process of development.

The British Museum exhibits a stone that has the imprint of a bird's foot. There was a time in the distant past when the material was soft and supple. Now it bears the marks of a moment when a creature walked all over it. How like us; crisis, pressure and conflict can leave their mark indelibly imprinted on our thinking.

As children we are impressionable, easily moulded, marred and sometimes scarred for life by bitter experiences. All of us have grown up with major influences on our lives. Experiences, education and environment are all powerful factors that leave their mark on our present perspective on life – some positive, others negative. These early imprints can easily become our later blueprints.

Babies are born with a thought process that is both uncluttered and unsophisticated.

Children quickly learn to monitor and eventually mimic those attitudes that form part of their surrounding environment. These attitudes are as susceptible to error as they are to truth. How often have we watched our children leave the safe environment of home to attend their first days at school, only to return with a different attitude? The swear word or unacceptable pattern of behaviour at the meal table all too often signals the end of childhood innocence. Yet school alone is not responsible for this. Yes, the school playground influences our children's attitudes, but the major player, at least when it comes to learned beliefs and behaviour, is the home. Parents are the primary shapers of a child's attitudes. The imprints we receive in childhood set the blueprints for what we do in adult life.

To some degree we are all shaped by our past, characterized and affected by people and events that have influenced our growing-up process. When the imprints in our childhood have been damaging and hurtful, we do not have to be forever bound by these wounds or by the attitudes they forged in us. Through spiritual rebirth and the indwelling Holy Spirit, each person can live free of these internalized restrictions. The gospel of Jesus Christ presents us with the dynamic possibility of realigning our thought patterns and shaking off the negative influences of our past.

The apostle Paul puts it powerfully in Ephesians 4:22-24:

> "With regard to your former way of life ... put off your old self, which is being corrupted by its deceitful desires ... be made new in the attitude of your minds; and ... put on the new self, created to be like God in true righteousness and holiness."

Rather than apportion blame on parents, the church or society, each of us must take full responsibility for our own attitudes. We need to acknowledge and then adjust any wrong thinking we may have. Like the members of the church in Corinth, we must align our thinking with God's and this requires that we "demolish arguments and every pretension that sets itself up against the knowledge of God, and we take captive every thought to make it obedient to Christ" (2 Corinthians 10:5).

How Attitudes are Formed

If the secret of a successful life is in monitoring and maintaining healthy attitudes, what are the main characteristics of an attitude? All mental attitudes have three main components: belief, feeling and action. These cover almost everything we think, feel, say or do. What I believe about a person, object or event will predetermine how I feel, and how I feel affects my course of action.

Let's look at these three components.

Beliefs are based on facts, generalizations, prejudices, stereotypes, experiences and assumptions. They form the basis of every attitude and become the key factor in determining and changing the behaviours that we exhibit.

Change a person's beliefs and you will undoubtedly change his or her behaviour.

The mind is a fortified stronghold that incorporates countless arguments, theories, prejudicial ideas and fantasies. These help to predetermine the way we approach any given situation and our response to it. The English word "believe" comes from an Anglo-Saxon word that means to "be-live". The same Solomon we criticized earlier wrote, "As [a man] thinks within himself, so he is" (Proverbs 23:7, NASB). In other words, our lives are not the product of what we eat or wear, but what we think and believe.

Over the passage of time, our minds create a "frame of reference" – the internalized, learned patterns of thinking against which a new incoming experience is measured. It is these well-established fortifications that create a formidable opponent for any new thoughts, any invitations to change behaviour. "Our battle is to bring down every deceptive fantasy and every imposing defence that men erect against the true knowledge of God. We fight to capture every thought until it acknowledges the authority of Christ" (2 Corinthians 10:5, JBP). Beliefs are therefore the basic component of an attitude. What we believe as factual (whether it is true or not) affects the way we act or react.

Beliefs predetermine our favourable or unfavourable response to people, objects or events.

Based on the facts available to us, be they true, false or invented, we all formulate certain attitudes. A rumour can be true or false, but if we give it room in our thought process it will alter our angle of approach accordingly. For instance, if like the ancient mariners we believe the world was flat, and to venture too far from the shoreline risks us falling off the face of the world into oblivion, we will never lose sight of the coastline!

Each of us has a set of beliefs concerning life. Built over a period of years, they are the result of various environmental, educational and experiential factors. If you grew up in a negative environment, being continually told you would never amount to much will probably have created beliefs about yourself that make it difficult for you to see yourself as a winner. With such a negative approach to life, every new venture is perceived as being fraught with problems and a pathway to probable disaster.

Our inability to enter the dynamic adventure of the Christian life is often rooted in a devaluation of our position in Christ. This inability to see by faith our redemptive worth

– as reflected in the mirror of God's Word – cripples spiritual effectiveness. If we choose to focus on the negative and make wrong comparisons, we envisage ourselves as misfits having little use in God's eternal purposes. Winners are people who have learned to maintain high levels of expectation in the face of opposing factors.

Feelings follow from these beliefs. Facts, when sown into a fertile mind, seldom remain as inactive knowledge. As they germinate in the ground of personal insecurities, believed facts produce either favourable or unfavourable feelings towards people, objects and events. These perceived facts cause us to develop likes or dislikes that cause us to respond positively or react negatively.

Yet, feelings on their own cannot be trusted. They are as unstable as water, fluctuating according to our mood, state of health and external conditions.

Negative feelings are often the result of first- or second-hand experiences and become the personal lens through which we view life.

If the beliefs that these feelings are based on are skewed, faulty or harmful, then the feelings they produce will be the same.

For instance, it is possible to prejudge a stranger solely on the beliefs created through the words of a third person – be they true or false. These harmful beliefs produce a crop of feelings towards the individual that may or may not be based in reality. Racism is a classic example of this kind of prejudicial thinking. Racial prejudice is an unhealthy attitude built on a wrong set of beliefs. When we embrace wrong beliefs about people from a different culture, about people of a different skin colour, these wrong beliefs produce negative feelings of mistrust, fear, hatred, anger and even violence. Feelings therefore form a pivotal point in the three component parts of an attitude.

A Christian is someone who has chosen to live in God's kingdom. This kingdom is a kingdom of "righteousness". This means being in a right relationship with God and believing and doing the right things, according to God's measure of right and wrong. When a person bases their lives on these beliefs, this influences their feelings. They begin to experience *affectively* what they have embraced *cognitively*. They start, in other words, to feel the feelings that are characteristic of this kingdom. Among many other godly affections, this includes "righteousness, peace and joy in the Holy Spirit" (Romans 14:17). Positive beliefs, in other words, lead to positive feelings.

Actions. Someone has aptly said: "Ten per cent of life is what happens to me; 90 per cent is how I react."[24] Our beliefs produce a range of feelings that in turn cause a chain reaction of either positive or negative actions. It is therefore essential to build our attitudes on godly beliefs. King David wrote: "Let the words of my mouth and the meditation of my heart be acceptable in Your sight, O LORD, my rock and my Redeemer" (Psalm 19:14, NASB). The Hebrew word for "heart" includes the mind, will, emotions or feelings. Sadly, David failed to live according to his own code of practice. He wrongly believed that he himself was exempt from battle "at the time when kings go off to war" (2 Samuel 11:1). David then allowed his feelings for another man's wife to get out of control. Eventually, his desire for Bathsheba led him into a series of events that tragically resulted in an act of adultery and then murder.

You see? What you believe affects how you behave.

You can send an army of advisers to teach Developing countries the economic and social benefits of birth control,

---

24. Charles R. Swindoll, *Strengthening Your Grip: Essentials in an Aimless World* (Word, 1983).

but without the removal of wrong ethnic barriers and religious beliefs, the whole exercise will prove futile. Once triggered, beliefs and feelings have a domino effect on our social conduct.

With the resurgence of neo-Nazi, anti-Semitic and anti-immigration beliefs, it seems that blatant racism is back. The hostility and hatred of those who embrace a white supremacist ideology is escalating. Here is a classic case of wrong beliefs leading to harmful feelings. But these feelings do not always remain internalized. In an age when people can say pretty well anything they like on social media, negative feelings lead to destructive words. These in turn lead to harmful actions.

Negative Beliefs

Attitudes are like magistrates sitting in judgment on the events of life. They are silent observers that look at and listen to life's circumstances, poised to bring judgment at any given moment.

Attitudes are like spectacles; they are the lenses through which we view things. As a result, they affect our perspective on life.

Having finished my Bible college training, I was assigned to my first pastorate. Still wet behind the proverbial ears, I had no idea what to expect. My first challenge was a young lad called Peter. Why, I wondered, did young Peter behave the way he did? A pleasant five-year-old, he persistently hid behind his mother whenever I tried to hold a conversation with his parents. When I visited their home, I would enter the front door only to see young Peter making a speedy exit from the room. He wouldn't reappear until long after my departure. What was wrong? It wasn't just a bad dose of shyness. It seemed that I was the only one he treated in this manner.

I tried every way I knew to establish some level of friendship with Peter, but to no avail. I had to find out who had the problem – him or me. At the end of one Sunday-morning meeting, I decided to confront the issue. I drew his parents aside and broached the issue of Peter's pastoral phobia.

"Excuse me for asking, but could you tell me why it is your son reacts like he does whenever he sees me?"

"Oh," his father replied. "Don't worry about that. It's just our Peter."

"But I am concerned. I'd really like to resolve this issue."

"Well," the mother said, feeling somewhat embarrassed and a little ashamed. "Every time Peter is naughty, we tell him that if he doesn't behave, we'll lock him in the cupboard and send for the pastor."

There was my answer!

No wonder the lad behaved the way he did. He viewed me as punishment personified. I had become the ultimate threat used by two irresponsible parents who were unable to bring the right kind of correction to their five-year-old son. Peter had been fed certain information through which he had formed a set of beliefs. These beliefs triggered strong feelings which in turn became a driving force that caused him to take evasive action.

Attitudes are made up of beliefs, which in turn create feelings, that in turn result in either a positive or a negative course of action.

Attitudes represent an individual's readiness to either respond positively or react negatively. They are predetermined patterns of thinking that affect the way we act or react to a given situation. Faced with the same set of circumstances, one person will act in one way, while another person might act totally differently. It's all a question of attitude.

There's Music at the Top

Of all the symphonic sounds heard from heaven, the first eleven verses of Matthew chapter 5 are a musical masterpiece. Here is a "Heavenly Octave" that resonates with the fatherly heart of God. Here are eight symphonic sounds that create an octanoic scale, heaven's design for Christian living. Each note is not only individually crucial but sequentially vital to what goes before and after. Together they represent a Christ-like character which, when played out in everyday life, will lead to a crescendo of heavenly applause.

To hear this symphony, you need to be prepared to climb. *Life on the Hill* is a study of what Jesus taught His climbing companions (Matthew 5:1-2) – lessons imperative to authentic Christian living in God's alternative society – the Kingdom of Heaven on the earth.

Climbers are a strange breed. The desire to climb is only surpassed by a passion to reach the top. Here they may pause to appreciate life on a different level, before commencing their descent.

Remember, the summit is just a halfway point. The descent is often where mistakes are made, where disaster happens.

So, if you're ready, let's grab our gear and go climbing.

GROUP DISCUSSION AND PERSONAL APPLICATION GUIDE

Group Discussion:

- As a fun group activity, why not encourage everyone to make a paper airplane and then organize a collective test flight. Discussion points around a correct or incorrect "angle of approach" to people, objects and events are numerous.

- Like the story of Peter, are there any fears or anxieties that you have learnt from your parents?

Personal Application:

- In terms of my beliefs, am I still living in an old time zone?

- What changes is God asking me to make in the light of this chapter?

When it comes to Personal Application we would encourage you to involve a "Spiritual Summiteer" (see page 37) so as to give yourself some level of accountability and guide you on your ongoing journey.

IT'S TIME TO CLIMB

"Raw dependence is the raw material out of which God performs His greatest miracles."

Mark Batterson, *The Circle Maker* [25]

---

25. Mark Batterson, *The Circle Maker*, (Zondervan, 2011), p. 15.

BE-ATTITUDE 1

*"You're blessed when you're at the end of your rope.
With less of you, there is more of God and his rule."* [26]

A non-selfish angle of approach to life whereby
we acknowledge our total dependence on God
and our interdependence on other people.

---

26. Matthew 5:3, *The Message*

5

RICH MAN, POOR MAN

*"Have this attitude in yourselves
which was also in Christ Jesus . . .
He . . . emptied Himself." [27]*

At the height of British Colonialism, an English traveller arrives in Africa determined to get to his destination as quickly as possible. "He charters some local porters to carry his supplies. After an exhausting day of travel, all on foot, and a fitful night's sleep, he gets up to continue the journey. But the porters refuse. Exasperated, he begins to cajole, bribe, plead, but nothing works. They will not move an inch. Naturally, he asks why. Answer was. 'They are waiting for their souls to catch up with their bodies.'"[28]

Time Out

Although some parents might see the idiom "time out" as a form of discipline, the phrase was first made popular in the game of basketball where it referred to a short period of time during which the game is suspended so that players can rest as the coach talks tactics. Time out in this original meaning is an opportunity to get everyone on the same page, as coaches call for actions which they believe will influence the outcome of the game.

---

27. Philippians 2:5-7, NASB.
28. John Mark Comer, *The Ruthless Elimination of Hurry* (Hodder & Stoughton, 2019).

Jesus took time out during His ministry. We read in Matthew 5:1-2 (MSG):

"When Jesus saw his ministry drawing huge crowds, he climbed a hillside. Those who were apprenticed to him, the committed, climbed with him. Arriving at a quiet place, he sat down and taught his climbing companions."

Midway through a busy itinerary, while experiencing unprecedented popularity, Jesus called "time out". Stepping away from the field of play, He separated His team from the crowd and begins to talk tactics. In the pursuit of a worthy goal, we can forget the importance of allowing time for "our soul to catch up with our body".

When I am panicked by a seemingly endless "to do" list, my wife often encourages me to remember the words of the prophet who wrote, "He that believeth, shall not make haste" (Isaiah 28:16, KJV). There are moments in life when, for the sake of our physical, emotional and spiritual well-being, we all need to press the pause button, to stop the game and listen to some heavenly tactics. And if *Life on the Hill* is not to be relegated to a mere rerun of "The Grand old Duke of York", we will need to exercise what John Mark Comer calls *The Ruthless Elimination of Hurry*. Without this, our reading exercise will become nothing more than a carbon copy of the ageing Duke of York's pointless exercise of marching troops up and down a hillside, without ever engaging the enemy.

To truly listen and learn from the tactics Jesus gives His team, we will first need to follow in the footsteps of Jesus – to step away from our busy schedule and create a moment of quiet meditation for our soul to catch up with our body. Once there, we need to ask ourselves a fundamental question: How desperate am I for God?

We live in an environment where positive confession masquerades as spiritual faith, where Sunday attendance is synonymous with spirituality, where spiritual disciplines are regarded as an optional extra, and where social herding has created a crowd rather than a community. Our fallen, consumerist culture has the power to dissipate our zeal for the eternal and create a casual rather than a committed form of Christianity.

It's time for the Body of Christ to once again experience *holy desperation – holy* because it is born of the Holy Spirit, and *desperate* because it makes us restless and reckless for all things godly.

A seed of godly discontent, given time, will germinate and grow into holy desperation. This will undoubtedly create a desire to let go of the temporal to attain the eternal.

Sadly, too many Christians are more likely to be consumers of the temporal than consumed by the eternal. We need to remember the heroes of the faith and the protagonists of revival history. Holy desperation caused Jacob to wrestle with God (Genesis 22:22-32), Rachel to cry, "Give me children, or I'll die" (Genesis 30:1) and Smith Wigglesworth (the Bradford plumber who became a mighty man of God) to say, "The secret of spiritual success is a hunger that persists. It is an awful condition to be satisfied with one's spiritual attainments. God was and is looking for hungry, thirsty people."[29]

The Bible is full of desperate people, those willing do almost anything in the pursuit of a loving heavenly Father. Like the woman with a blood condition in Mark 5:25-34, desperate people push through the crowd. Forgetting religious protocol, those thirsty for God find a way to run through those who want to push back on their dream.

Holy desperation wrecks you for anything less than God's best. It is an inner cry of the soul – a tear-jerking, heart-wrenching, soul-searching activity that makes us reckless and ruthless in our pursuit of the holy. It cannot be forced, demanded, cajoled or legislated. Holy desperation is an inner brokenness birthed out of a deep, inconsolable and uncontrollable passion for a higher level of spiritual life.

Before we take one more step, we need to call "time out" on our busy lives and ask ourselves one pressing question.

How desperate am I for God?

Base Camp

As the clouds clear and we catch a glimpse of the summit, the enormity of the task before us begins to dawn. *Life on the Hill* is no stroll in the park but a radical commitment to life at a different level – a climb that no one should undertake lightly.

---

29. Quoted in Nestor Kouassi, *The Coming Deluge of His Glory* (Westbow Press, 2019), chapter 6.

If we allow the Word of God to work in us, the expedition we are about to undertake will wreck us for anything less. We marvel at the four Be-Attitudes that teach us to how to *rely* on God. Each of these will mess with our brains and play havoc with our self-sufficiency. At times, the severity of this steep learning curve will become deeply challenging, but for those determined to engage the enemy, rather than indulge in a rerun of "The Grand Old Duke of York", this promises to be a life-changing experience.

As we prepare to climb, we should remember that God's kingdom is an upside-down kingdom where the least become the greatest, the last are first, maturity comes from being childlike, the weak are strong and the poor become strangely rich (Luke 14:11; Matthew 18:1-6; 2 Corinthians 12:10; Matthew 5:3). As such, each of these eight Be-Attitudes represents a counter-cultural reality; they are not some figment of man's imagination, nor are they mere natural tendencies present in some people, absent in others. These are attitudes available to everyone who becomes "partakers of the divine nature" (2 Peter 1:4, NASB). They are family traits that should be evident in every born-again believer. They are eight attainable goals for which God "has given us everything we need" (2 Peter 1:3).

Challenging our beliefs and changing our behaviour, each Be-Attitude is counter cultural. They are kingdom rules of life.

As if to emphasize that, Jesus bookends His heavenly octave with the phrase, "Theirs [and theirs only] is the kingdom."[30]

---

30. Matthew 5:3,10. If the primary emphasis in each of these Be-Attitudes is on the word "blessed", the secondary emphasis is most certainly on the words "theirs" and "they". In the original Greek, the emphatic pronoun is used: "theirs and theirs only". So, for example, "Blessed are the pure in heart, for they [and they only] will see God."

Those who live like Jesus, who embrace the Be-Attitudes, belong to the Kingdom.

So, let's begin the ascent.

In true mountaineering style, Jesus establishes a base camp in what He calls "poverty of spirit". This becomes the foundation for all that follows, a supply chain from which committed climbers will need to draw resources to complete both their ascent and descent. Those who are desperate for the kingdom will climb to the summit and then descend to the valleys. They will draw from God's resources and relate to other people, like Jesus, in a way that is different from the world's standards. This attitude of being desperate for God, wrecked for anything other than His presence, is the place where we begin. It is Base Camp. But it is not just a place that we visit; it's a place we are called to inhabit. This is true for all eight of the Be-Attitudes. In God's upside-down kingdom, you cannot experience fulness without first knowing emptiness.

How different is the curriculum in God's School of the Spirit – different, anyway, from any known modules in the colleges of human learning! While humanity majors in self-sufficient beliefs and self-assertive behaviour, treating interpersonal relationships as a means to an end, kingdom living is the opposite. If we are to experience true satisfaction, we must first attend Class 101 on divine dependency.

Poverty of Spirit

By comparing the two versions of the Sermon on the Mount (Matthew 5:3/Luke 6:20), some have mistakenly understood that Jesus was advocating *material* poverty as a means of spiritual blessing. They have wrongly thought that Jesus was teaching that a lack of worldly wealth is essential for receiving divine grace. Commenting on this, William Barclay writes, "We must be careful not to think that this beatitude calls actual material poverty a good thing. Poverty is not a good thing. Jesus would never have called 'blessed' a state where people live in slums and have not enough to eat, and where health rots because conditions are all against it. That kind of poverty it is the aim of the Christian gospel to remove."[31] Jesus therefore did not want us to embrace a poverty mentality that views excellence as worldly, and the inferior as acceptable. Such an attitude would give the impression that Christians do not care about doing things well.

A mindset that refuses to accept excellence as a means of promoting heaven's kingdom on earth is a proverbial shot in the foot for the Body of Christ.

Although poverty is not an indicator of our disobedience or a mark of divine disapproval, it can have a beneficial effect. Hunger can sharpen our desire for both the natural and the supernatural, and the absence of material wealth can increase our dependency on a loving heavenly Father (Matthew 6:30-34; Luke 6:20).

The day my father purchased his first new car was one I'll not forget. After years of suffering the problems of cheap second-hand vehicles, he decided to buy the car of his dreams. With shining chrome work and smart, white-walled tyres, this beautiful yellow-and-black 1959 Ford Consul was everything he had dreamed. With its imitation leopard-skin seat covers (a 1950s thing!), this vehicle was impressive. Imagine my surprise when, having driven the vehicle home and reversed it into the garage, Dad decided to leave it there undriven for three months!

---

31. William Barclay, *The Daily Study Bible* (St Andrew Press, 1978).

As my mentor in giving, my father taught me the importance and implications of honouring God with our finances. "Those who honour God," he declared, "would in turn be honoured." Seeing his business grow was therefore not a surprise because Dad honoured God with his tithes and offerings. Nevertheless, buying a flashy new car and then hiding it from public view was not my idea of fun.

Somehow, Dad was unable to balance the blessings of prosperity with the belief that others would see his gain as customer exploitation. Public opinion and the fear of others made it difficult for Dad to enjoy the goodness of God. So, there the car sat, and we had to be satisfied with an occasional sneak under the cover of darkness and a pretend ride in a stationary vehicle.

Total Destitution

The poverty that Jesus is advocating is a poverty of spirit.[32] This is an internal condition that changes everything. It is an inside-out way of looking at life. How different this is from the world's way of thinking! The humanist says, "Improve the environment and you will eventually improve the person." Jesus begins at the centre of our lives and works out to the circumference. He teaches in the first of the Be-Attitudes that it is being spiritually desperate that changes everything.

The New Testament writers use two words to describe poverty. The first is the Greek noun *penes* which was often used to describe a labourer who is barely existing from day to day. To miss a day's work is to miss a day's meals.

The second is the adjective *ptochos* which means "poor as a beggar, destitute". This is the word Jesus uses. He is therefore not talking about being materially poor but spiritually desperate. He is also not talking about having a low standard of living but an acute, intense, abject desperation for God. Those who are spiritually destitute exercise an angle of approach to life that is completely dependent on God's grace and goodness. Such an attitude flies in the face of independence and self-sufficiency. It is truly counter-cultural.

Dependent and Interdependent

The self-sufficient philosophy of the humanist regards God as irrelevant for the survival and ascent of humanity. Such self-exaltation stands in direct opposition to God. When humanity

---

32. When written as "Spirit" (capitalized), it normally refers to the Holy Spirit. Where we find "spirit" (lower case), it is often best understood as attitude, as here in Matthew 5:3. Also, 1 Corinthians 4:21 ("a gentle spirit"); 2 Corinthians 4:13 ("spirit of faith"); Ephesians 4:23 ("spirit of your mind" NASB), which NIV translates as, "attitude of your minds". The spirit of a person is that inner part of their being that relates to God. John 4:24: "God is spirit, and his worshippers must worship in spirit and in truth." Men and women relate to God from their spirit, and vice versa: "The Spirit himself testifies with our spirit that we are God's children" (Romans 8:16).

rejects God as King, everyone does what is right in their own eyes (Judges 21:25). Such thinking treats God as nothing more than a spare tyre, to be used only in an emergency.

At the heart of the working relationship between God the Father, Son and Holy Spirit we find interdependence rather than independence. Jesus repeatedly pointed out that His power and authority were rooted in a healthy dependence on His Father. Without grasping for position or recognition, Jesus emptied Himself, took on the role of a servant, laid down His life and became totally obedient to His Father's will.

This total dependence on the Father is not only a picture of what it means to be poor in spirit; it is an example that we are all called to follow. The apostle Paul says that, "Your attitude should be the same as that of Christ Jesus . . ." (Philippians 2:5) who "for your sakes . . . became poor, so that you through his poverty might become rich" (2 Corinthians 8:9). Jesus Christ left the glory of heaven, laid aside the attributes of divinity, and in His human flesh became completely reliant on God, through the power and presence of the Holy Spirit. In other words, as a human being, He became empty in order that He might be filled, and thereby established, as the Son of God by nature, the path and pattern for all sons and daughters of God by adoption.

For us to follow His lead requires a mental reset in which we surrender our attitude of prideful independence and worldly self-sufficiency, becoming instead totally dependent on God as our source of supply.

But this isn't the only implication of the first Be-Attitude.

The flipside of the same coin is that we are rightly dependent on others.

The early church exercised an attitude of dependence on God and interdependence on each other.

The Christ followers who became desperate for the Holy Spirit before Pentecost are an example to us of self-emptying and abandonment to God's power and strength. These same believers, both before and after Pentecost, were also interdependent. Their interpersonal relationships were not merely based on corporate activities, but also on a commitment to value and care for each other. As we read at the end of Acts 4, "All the believers were one in heart and mind. No one claimed that any of his possessions was his own, but they shared everything they had" (Acts 4:32). Dependence on God and interdependence on each other were hallmarks of the earliest church. When we are "poor in spirit", we recognize not only our need for God, but our need for each other.[33]

Lessons from Nature

We see this pattern in the natural world. Although some humanists teach that humans are an end in themselves, in nature things are different; everything has an inbuilt two-fold code of self-identification (individuality) and corporate integration (interdependence). For instance, a human cell knows its individual function while at the same time recognizing its need of others for the sake of the whole body. How does a kidney cell know it's not a heart cell? It's a mystery. Each cell knows its identity, yet it does not become independent. Rather, it arranges itself in the body for the benefit of the whole. When cells do act independently, the body becomes sick. Within each cell is "a rugged individuality which can go on a rampage and break laws – as cancer cells do".[34] Quartzes, electrons, neutrons, molecules and galaxies all function with this same two-fold code. Recognizing their individual uniqueness and identity,

---

33. See Philippians 4:13; Romans 8:37, Psalm 87:7, NASB.
34. Ron Trudinger, *Cells for Life* (Kingsway Publications, 1983).

they still fit into God's larger economy. Everything follows the same two-fold pattern. A note separated out from a musical scale becomes a dreary monotone. A typed character divorced from a word becomes a meaningless symbol. If a colour deserts its spectrum, it loses its beauty. If a star forsakes its orbit, it destroys itself.

God has made human beings the same way, as unique individuals, and yet as interdependent beings. When we start acting in unity, this does not mean uniformity but rather conformity to the likeness of Jesus. While we still maintain our individual identity, we must look for our personal fulfilment in a relationship of total dependence on our loving heavenly Father and in meaningful relationships with our brothers and sisters in Christ. Human beings are not an end in themselves; we find our place and purpose within the Body of Christ. As part of an authentic community, God's alternative society, we learn to be givers not takers, people who thrive in an interdependent role where collaboration matters. We live constantly in an environment in which our individuality is not overwhelmed or submerged by tasks, and where our interdependence is celebrated through teamwork.

Unteachable Individualists

Personal insecurity breeds independence. When left unhealed, it creates an intense desire for isolation. While introverts might see imposed isolation as a dream scenario, left unchecked, this self-isolation will build an independent spirit that becomes the antithesis of what Jesus meant by being "poor in spirit". We need God, and we need each other. God has not called Christians to isolationism. There is no such thing as solitary religion, as John Wesley rightly warned us. The Church is called to be the salt of the earth, the light of the world, a city on a hill that cannot be hidden and the joy of the whole earth.[35]

The spiritual Lone Ranger, who drifts in and out of local church life, is answerable to no one. Such an individual often finds personal discipleship difficult and will display some, if not all, the following marks of an unteachable person:

- Values only his or her own opinion and turns God's Word into his/her own ideas.
- Relies on personal ability and resources rather than obeys the call to change.
- Gives a display of hurt feelings.
- Pulls apart any advice given to them.
- Becomes argumentative when challenged.
- Raises other issues as a smokescreen to cloud the real problem.
- Feels he or she is a special case.
- Exhibits stubbornness.
- Sees themselves as more important than others.
- Feels got at and hard done by.
- Looks for an alternative explanation to the one offered.
- Only submits when routed on every argument.

Poor in Spirit, Forceful in Faith

Now that we have established this fundamental kingdom attitude, we can move forward and begin to exercise godly authority over what is, thanks to the finished work of Christ, legally ours. When we exercise an angle of approach to life characterized by the term "poor in spirit", then ours is the kingdom.

---

35. Matthew 5:13-14; Psalms 48:2.

To the natural mind, poverty of spirit and inheriting the kingdom may seem poles apart. Yet they are inseparable.

When living under God's authority as His dependents, we are empowered to exercise authority (Luke 7:2-10). Christians are called to be active in bringing the Kingdom of Heaven to earth.

While some wait for things to happen, the poor in spirit make things happen. Poor in spirit but forceful in faith, they bring heaven's rule to earth through the power of God's Spirit. This requires us to have the same radical attitude seen in Joshua and Caleb (Numbers 14); we must not be willing to settle for anything less than our full inheritance in health, finances, work, home and family. We are called to conquer circumstances, not merely cope with them. When faced with any situation calculated to rob us, this attitude causes us to stand boldly and by "the abundance of grace and . . . the gift of righteousness reign in life through the One, Jesus Christ." (Romans 5:17, NASB).

At the age of forty, Moses was a man educated in all the wisdom of the Egyptians and powerful in speech and action. Yet he lacked "poverty of spirit". He relied on his own strength and reasoning and used the forcefulness of human aggression and assertiveness. Having murdered an Egyptian, he "thought that his own people would realize that God was using him to rescue them, but they did not" (Acts 7:22-25). So, he fled in fear and became an exile in Midian for forty years.

How different is the man who later approached the burning bush on Mount Horeb! The experience in the School of the Desert had by then created in him a different angle of approach to life. This one-time independent individual was now totally dependent on God and interdependent with others. He humbly inquired of God, "Who am I that I should go to Pharaoh and bring the Israelites out of Egypt?" (Exodus 3:11).

But the man who was now "poor in spirit" was about to become forceful in faith. Laying down his shepherd's staff, which in turn became a serpent, Moses initially fled from it, as he had run from a crisis forty years earlier. But God commanded him to grasp it by its tail (Exodus 4:4, NASB). This required faith in God's Word. Moses's obedience turned a shepherd's staff into a kingly sceptre, a symbol of rule with which he would extend God's purposes on the earth. In the same way, those who know a poverty of spirit can expect the fulfilment of the promise, "Theirs is the kingdom."

GROUP DISCUSSION AND PERSONAL APPLICATION GUIDE

Group Discussion:

- How can we practically avoid this book becoming a rerun of "The Grand Old Duke of York"?

- What does *take time out* look like for you?

- How do you understand the phrase "poor in spirit"?

- Do you have any workable suggestions on how to reset the balance between independence and interdependence within the Christian community?

- For those group leaders able to do this, why not encourage your group to take 30 minutes in the next week to spend quality time with God. As leaders you might want to offer help in terms of looking after children, cooking a meal or shopping, etc. Then in your next group meeting encourage people to share what they experienced in their time out.

Personal Application:

- When asked the question "Are you desperate for God?" how would you answer and how should you act on the answer?

- Check out the list of unteachable characteristics. Are there any of these characteristics in your life? If you're brave enough, ask someone you trust and who believes in you to listen to your answers.

When it comes to Personal Application we would encourage you to involve a "Spiritual Summiteer" (see page 37) so as to give yourself some level of accountability and guide you on your ongoing journey.

BE-ATTITUDE 2

"Blessed are those who mourn, for they will be comforted."

A readiness to be broken with what breaks God's
heart and a willingness to co-labour with heaven
to restore what has been lost on the earth.

6

GOOD GRIEF

"Have we no tears for revival?"
Leonard Ravenhill[36]

I will never forget the day God interrupted the programme at a conference I was attending. I was about to hear a session on corporate prayer. Having prayed with the church leaders before, I thought I had a good idea about what that might contain. However, before the session began, a young leader was permitted to speak. As he opened his mouth, it was obvious he was deeply moved. With a voice broken by the gravity of what God had shown him, he described a graphic picture of the Church. He painted with broad brushstrokes a picture of a malformed, emaciated and immature Church, having a childlike body and an adult head. He struggled to compose himself, as tears streamed down his face. His plea was that the delegates would call to God on behalf of the Church, to pray that the Holy Spirit would convict the Body of Christ to grow up.

His words pierced through the façade of religious formalism and cancelled our prearranged agenda. Cut to the quick, grown men began to fall to the ground in tears, calling on God. People started to pray earnestly. Soon the tears turned to loud crying, wailing and deep groaning. A tsunami of emotion broke upon the gathered crowd. The united cry intensified with every passing minute, as wave after wave of godly sorrow swept through the hall.

---

36. Leonard Ravenhill, *Revival God's Way* (Bethany House, 2006 Edition), p. 69.

The morning of prayer had turned into a prayer of mourning!

Before that session I thought I knew about prayer, but that morning changed me. My preconceived ideas about corporate prayer were shattered. The experience left a deep and lasting impression that remains with me today. That session took my understanding of prayer to a whole new level. Having been brought up in Charismatic circles, I had experienced noise and emotion, but never anything like this. In all my years of meeting and praying with Holy Spirit-filled leaders, this was new and uncharted territory. We had tapped into the heart of the Father and, for one moment, we were sharing His grief.

Still enveloped in this godly environment, I found myself asking God for some form of clarification, muttering under my breath questions like, "What is all this?" "What's happening here?"

Immediately, I sensed a heavenly response to my earthly quandary.

"This is mourning."

With that, I understood. We had become aggrieved with what grieves the heart of God. We were broken by what breaks God's heart. I was experiencing what Jesus wanted His followers to experience when He shared the second of His Be-Attitudes: "Blessed are those who mourn, for they shall be comforted" (Matthew 5:4).

Mourning has Broken

Of all the eight Be-Attitudes, "Blessed are those who mourn" has caused me more difficulty than any other.

How could Jesus consider someone happy when they were enduring the trauma of bereavement?

How could He declare that someone suffering the loss of a loved one was fortunate? The sorrowful intercession at the conference changed all that. Up until that time, I had often used this Be-Attitude as sermon material for the occasional funeral. "Jesus wants to comfort those who mourn." Sounds helpful, doesn't it?

Sometimes what is helpful isn't necessarily right. Having experienced first-hand the mournful praying at the conference, I realized that I had misinterpreted this Be-Attitude and was consequently asking all the wrong questions. Thinking originally that the verse applied to bereaved people at funerals, I was confused. How was it possible to picture a mourner as someone to be envied? How can we view bereavement as a joyful experience? Was I to congratulate the bereaved on their sense of loss? Surely not. Jesus would never condone such a callous idea. I had become stuck in my thinking. Interpreting the Be-Attitude as a word of comfort to the bereaved, I had run into a contradiction. If the word "mourning" applies to death, sorrow, anguish, tears and loss, then Jesus was contradicting what the Bible elsewhere teaches. The Kingdom of Heaven, after all, is a kingdom of "righteousness, peace and joy in the Holy Spirit" (Romans 14:17) not a place of sorrow.

The conference session created a paradigm shift, one that cleared the fog of confusion and brought bright rays of revelation. I saw for the first time that *mourning* here refers to those moments when we are so in touch with the Father heart of God that we feel what He feels. Our hearts bleed just as His heart bleeds. Our eyes fill just as His do. When we intercede with tears and groans, we are closer to the Father than we will ever know, and He is closer to us than we will ever know too, because His Word tells us that He is near to the broken-hearted. In His kingdom, those who mourn refers to those who are in such deep and desperate need for Him that they weep when He weeps. To those people, engaged in truly authentic prayer, He promises divine comfort.

How counter-cultural this is! Truly, Jesus challenges every aspect of human behaviour.

Far from endorsing apathy or compassion fatigue, He urges us to look at the world through the eyes of His Son.

He woos us by His Holy Spirit into uttering sighs that are too deep for words as we see the powerlessness and sinfulness of a sleeping Church, and the desperate longing and suffering of an awakening world. He invites people into this sacred space of oneness with His divine heart, incentivizing us with the promise that we will be happy people if we mourn, comforted when we cry. How different His kingdom is from any other! In this upside-down culture of heaven, the happiest people on the earth are those who are most moved with sorrow for the things that grieve God.

Perhaps, now, the reality of *Life on the Hill* is beginning to dawn. There is a cost to this kind of spirituality, but there are rewards too. The cost is in the tears we shed in the night, but the reward is in the joy we feel in the morning. Those who sob as God sobs for the sins of the Church and the world may look like the most miserable of people, but they are what Charles Spurgeon called "happy saints"![37] They are those who live in a

---

37. See Mark Stibbe, *From Orphans to Heirs* (Oxford: BRF, 1999), pp. 115–116.

deep satisfaction of soul. While the world sings, "I can't get no satisfaction," these happy saints sing, "All is well with my soul." This Be-Attitude is therefore a Kingdom paradox. The more you weep, the happier you are!

While the mourning at the conference changed my understanding of this verse, I might not have needed that experience at all had I looked at the eight Be-Attitudes and realized that they are links in a chain, or steps on a stairway. Had I seen that being poor in spirit (step 1) leads directly to being mournful (step 2), I might have saved myself a lot of ... well, grief. Jesus was saying this: those who are spiritually destitute end up weeping. Those who are dependent on God and each other end up weeping as God weeps. They cry out in desperation to God to come, and they weep over the lack of His presence in their lives. They are happy because they end up satisfied, blessed and comforted.

A Grief Observed

Did Jesus have in mind the kind of wailing I saw in that session at the conference? Here we must acknowledge how influenced we are by the way people mourn in our culture.

From an Eastern perspective, mourning is often loud and wild. Emotions are not suppressed but released.

Bereavement is a very demonstrative and communal business. In Jesus's time, Eastern mourners used to tear their clothes and put on sackcloth or dirty garments – clothes calculated to cause the most irritation and personal discomfort. They would sprinkle ashes or dust on their heads to signify the devastation felt by the bereaved. Some would even sit among the ashes in the local garbage dump (Job 2:8). The mourner would not wash, eat or anoint themselves with oil for the period of mourning. Sometimes mourners would shave off their hair, leaving them unprotected from the sun's heat. How different it is in the Western world where death and mourning are a quiet, private affair. Westerners tend to embrace more of a "stiff upper lip" philosophy, a stoicism in which the legitimate and healthy expression of emotions is often tarnished as emotionalism.

In the Old Testament, we find that mourning is described in a graphic way as "howling like a jackal" or "moaning like an owl". Jesus was part of this Hebraic, Old Testament tradition. He was not so much a child of the Hellenistic philosophical world where aloofness was regarded as a virtue. In Jesus's life, mourning meant "loud and bitter cries of distress". It meant the kind of cries that Westerners would associate with a woman being raped, a civilian being abused by invading soldiers, a prisoner being tortured and isolated, a parent losing a child.[38] In the West, we are not used to such wailing. It is associated only with the most extreme traumas and abuses.

In the minds of those who sat listening to Jesus preaching the Sermon on the Mount, this must have sounded like a strange utterance. Mourning for them was not some quiet, joyful affair, but rather a visible, emotional demonstration of being utterly devastated. But Jesus was not referring to the sorrow and mourning that accompanies natural death. As with all these attitudes, the issue is a spiritual one. When He spoke of poverty and hunger, He was dealing with spiritual poverty and spiritual hunger. The kingdom of God is for the desperate. God comes in power and love to fill and embrace those who cry out, "I need You, God." He comes in revival fire to those who get on their faces and weep because they feel that they

---

38. Micah 1:8; Exodus 12:30; 2 Kings 2:12; Deuteronomy 22:23-27; Exodus 17:4; Genesis 27:34; 1 Samuel 4:10-14; Jeremiah 49:2; Isaiah 33:7; Lamentations 2:18.

have lost their first love for God, and as a result, mourn with loud cries the absence of the Lover of their souls. Perhaps, now, we understand. Jesus told us we will be happy in this condition. "You're blessed when you feel you've lost what is most dear to you" (Matthew 5:4, MSG).

To mourn is an angle of approach to life in which we are sensitive to and devastated by the loss of God's manifest presence and power in our lives and in the lives of others. Having come to a place where we are poor in spirit – desperate for more of God – we weep not only because we mourn the loss of the Father's love in our lives but also because we see the consequences of that loss in others. In this regard, the Be-Attitudes take us up to the heavenly realms to see our lives and the world from heaven's perspective. These attitudes, with the help of the Holy Spirit, lift us up so that we can live *Life on the Hill*. When I mourn on the summit, my whole being is taken up with a sense of loss. Food and sleep become unimportant. Whatever it takes to resolve this issue becomes food and drink to the mourner. It involves "passionate grief which leads to corresponding action".[39]

To mourn therefore means to be sensitive, inwardly broken, utterly devastated by a sense of loss.

It is not a formal, religious response to our need, or the need of others. It is the furthest remove from that, and from another common cultural phenomenon that was visible in Jesus's day – professional mourning. In New Testament times, some people had become so professional in the art of

---

39. Gerhard Kittel (ed.) and Gerhard Friedrich (ed.), *Theological Dictionary of the New Testament* (Eerdmans, 1976).

mourning that their expertise was hired to assist a family in times of grief. These people offered a kind of "Renta Mourn". It was professionals like these whom Jesus dismissed at the funeral of Jairus's daughter (Mark 5:38-40). Jesus had not come to condone such insincere patterns of behaviour, but to demonstrate the emotions that flowed from the heart of a loving heavenly Father.

Kingdom Sorrow

In this second Be-Attitude, Jesus is therefore not referring to "worldly sorrow", whose only result is "death". He is not speaking of formal laments or professional mourning. Nor is He speaking of a simple stirring of the emotions, though emotions are without question involved within this mourning (Matthew 27:3-4; Hebrews 12:16-17). Rather, Jesus is talking about a "godly sorrow [that] brings repentance" (2 Corinthians 7:8-11).

According to Paul's letter to the church at Corinth, this degree of sorrow is characterized by such things as:

- Eagerness to see the wrong corrected.
- Indignation at a violation of God's revealed will.
- Zeal to do God's will.
- Readiness to do whatever is necessary, to put things right.

To mourn, therefore, is to experience an interaction between God's Spirit and our spirit in which we see and sense a situation from God's viewpoint. Once we recognize a matter to be a violation of God's revealed will, we become so deeply affected by what we see that everything becomes expendable in the interests of change. Utterly devastated, we are ready, if necessary, to suffer personal inconvenience to bring divine order. Such feelings of utter devastation drive us to deal radically with ourselves and others.

Such grief motivates us to intercede on behalf of others, sometimes with tears and "groans that words cannot express" (Romans 8:26), with lamenting and wailing. It is a priestly activity whereby we partner with the Holy Spirit (Philippians 2:1) to grieve over what is not yet, but is still to come. If you think about it, when a person comes to Christ, they mourn over their sins. They grieve over a life lived without Jesus, over wasted time, over the absence of God in their thoughts. But this kind of mourning is not restricted to our conversion, as if it were something we experienced only once.

This angle of approach to life is not only fundamental to our new birth, it also plays a key role in our ongoing life in God's kingdom on the earth.

This, of course, comes at a cost. Godly sorrow will play havoc with our comfort zones. It will challenge our thinking and change our lifestyle. At the same time, it will motivate us to maintain a redemptive rather than an adversarial approach to people and events. We are not talking here about an emotional ego trip, as if mourning is a visible trophy of superior spirituality. Rather, mourning is an inner brokenness that arises from the indwelling nature of Christ. It causes us to wet our pillows with our tears as we realize just how much we, the Church, and the world miss the presence of God. In this respect, mourning adjusts our priorities. Mourners are no longer preoccupied with trivial pursuits, nor are they dependent on news outlets in seeing the world. Their one priority is crying out for more of God as they see themselves and others from the perspective of heaven. Living *Life on the Hill* resets the buttons. It re-establishes Kingdom agendas.

The Law of Brokenness

In revival history, every great move of God has been preceded and accompanied by this kind of grieving. One person wrote of the Welsh revival, "Such real travail of soul for the unsaved I have never before witnessed. I have seen young Evan Roberts convulsed with grief and calling on his audience to pray." Another added, "It was not the eloquence of Evan Roberts that broke men down, but his tears. He would break down, crying bitterly for God to bend them, in an agony of prayer, the tears coursing down his cheeks, with his whole frame writhing. Strong men would break down and cry like children. Women would shriek. A sound of weeping and wailing would fill the air. Evan Roberts in the intensity of his agony would fall in the pulpit, while many in the crowd often fainted."[40] This is a kind of supernatural law in the Kingdom of God. If you want to see a great spiritual harvest, you must first weep over your poverty in spirit and then mourn the loss of the manifest presence of God in your lives.

In this respect, the supernatural law resembles various natural laws.

In agriculture, the farmer must break up the land before sowing the seed that ends up bringing a great harvest. Similarly, in revivals, the hard soil of the heart must be broken up before there can be a great awakening.

In architecture, the builder will invariably have to pull something down or dig something up before erecting

---

40. Frank Bartleman, *What Really Happened at "Azusa Street"?* (Voice Christian Publishing, 1966).

something new. This is true in revivals as well. There often has to be a dismantling before there can be a re-mantling.

In short, brokenness always precedes blessing. As the psalmist wrote, "A broken and contrite heart, O God, you will not despise" (Psalm 51:17). It was only when the alabaster jar of expensive perfume was broken by the woman who had been saving it for her own burial that the aroma filled the room and the atmosphere changed. In the same manner, the selfless individual who pours out his or her life as unto the Lord becomes "a fragrant offering, an acceptable sacrifice, pleasing to God" (Philippians 4:18).

It is personal brokenness that changes spiritual atmospheres.

In both the Old and New Testaments, God seemingly specializes in taking the broken to demonstrate His eternal purpose. We read of broken vessels, a broken axe, a broken bone, broken ground, a broken bottle and broken bread.[41] In focusing on the broken, God illustrates His desire to use "the foolish things of the world to shame the wise; God chose the weak things of the world to shame the strong. He chose the lowly things . . . the despised things . . . the things that are not – to nullify the things that are, so that no-one may boast before him" (1 Corinthians 1:27-29). When we are broken – when we are spiritually destitute and weeping with desperation – then, when God brings about a great awakening, we cannot boast, because it is when we were empty and as nothing that He begins to work in power. Many great men and women of God carry the scars of past seasons

---

41. Judges 7:19-20; 2 Kings 6:1-6; Judges 15:14-17; 2 Kings 13:21; Hosea 10:12; Mark 14:3; Matthew 26:26.

of spiritual poverty and mourning but they consider them infinitely worthwhile because they are reminders of the price of revival.

Hardening of the Attitudes

In a world desensitized by the violence and horrors of social deprivation, it is easy to become callous and untouched by the catalogue of human tragedies that surround us. However, as citizens of God's kingdom, we are called to avoid this kind of emotional detachment. By God's grace, we are to maintain an attitude of spiritual sensitivity, to go on sensing the Holy Spirit's prompting and to continue to be grieved by what grieves the heart of God. We are to avoid becoming inwardly hard, having lost all sensitivity.

It is symptomatic of the age we live in to be unmoved by what moves the heart of God!

While some people may choose to cross the road to avoid humanity in need, the issues of racism, poverty, misogyny, homelessness, domestic violence, family breakdown and the ongoing refugee crisis need to be faced. What was it that made William Wilberforce work so hard for the abolition of slavery? Why did Lord Shaftesbury challenge the appalling conditions imposed by greedy managers on child labour in England? What caused Oliver Cromwell to stand against the demands of an earthly king, or David Brainerd to turn his back on wealth to spread the gospel? It was a spiritual sensitivity to the plight of their fellow men and women. Moved by the oppressive conditions of their day, they refused to distance themselves from contemporary social evils. These reformers rejected a Christian ghetto mentality and chose instead to practise a gospel that brought good news to the poor, freedom for prisoners, sight for the blind and release for the oppressed.

In his classic book *Tale of Three Kings: A Study in Brokenness*, Gene Edwards writes, "God has a university. It's a small school. Few enrol, even fewer graduate. Very, very few indeed. God has this school because he does not have broken men. Instead he has several other types of men. He has men who claim to be God's authority . . . and aren't; men who claim to be broken . . . and aren't. And men who are God's authority, but who are unbroken. And he has, regretfully, a spectroscopic mixture of everything in between. All of these he has in abundance; but broken men, hardly at all."[42]

This dreadful disease is called "the hardening of the heart" in the Bible. "Heart" here is used to describe the very centre of one's inner life. The heart is the fulcrum of all feeling. It is the seat of all emotions, desires and passions. It is the source of all thought and reflection, the seat of the will, the source of our resolve. Harbour a wrong attitude here and it is going to affect your whole life.

Once the heart becomes callous, insensitive, harsh and exacting, our whole life will produce bad fruit, affecting everyone we meet.

The hardening of the heart is a spiritual condition whose symptoms are obvious. The person whose heart has become hardened over time becomes callous, unyielding, stubborn, thick-skinned, hard, insensitive, unreceptive and lacking in sensitivity. This idea of "hardening" has a physical application too. Medically, the Greeks used the language of "hardening"

---

42. Gene Edwards, *A Tale of Three Kings: A Study in Brokenness* (Tyndale House Publishers; Reprint edition, 1992).

to describe the chalk stone that forms in the human joints, causing paralysis. The word was also used when speaking of a callus formed on a person's hand through digging or other similar manual activities. The word for hardening was later applied to a "loss of sensitivity or feeling", to, for instance, hardened skin that could not be penetrated by a needle. Later still, the Greek word was used to denote "an inability to see".

In both our physical and spiritual lives, becoming hardened is a dangerous and destructive thing. Who wants to have hardened joints, calluses or skin? And who wants to have a hardened heart. Hardening is toxic in both the natural and the supernatural dimensions of our lives. In the New Testament, a hard-hearted man or woman is someone who has become insensitive to the Holy Spirit and unable to perceive things from heaven's perspective.

You cannot live *Life on the Hill* with a hardened heart. Sooner or later, if you're to climb to the summit, you must let your heart be softened by the Holy Spirit, the ice must thaw in the fire of God's love, and you must start to feel what the weeping Father feels. There is no blessing for the one whose heart has become like stone.

Perhaps, at this point, it would be good to pray.

"Lord Jesus, help us to remain spiritually sensitive so that we grieve for what is grieving You. Move us to mourn when our first love wanes. Move us to mourn when others suffer. Move us to mourn when we grieve Your Spirit. Soften our callous hearts and dismantle the defences we have built up through the years. Lord, would You break up the fallow ground and rend the heavens and come down!"

Comfort Comes

Each Be-Attitude comes with a promise. For instance, the poor in spirit are promised the kingdom, the meek are promised they will inherit the earth, and so on. The promise accompanying this beatitude is that we will be comforted. Jesus assured His disciples that the Holy Spirit would be their "Comforter" or "Counsellor" – literally, "one called alongside to help" (John 14:16).

The blessing reserved for those who mourn is the comfort of the Holy Spirit's loving presence.

When we grieve that we have lost the manifest presence of God in our lives, and our grief is sincere, then the Spirit comes, bringing comfort.

Some people try to find a solace in ways other than mourning. They seek to forget, ignore or excuse their spiritual crises. Instead of mourning the loss of the sense of God's pleasure and power, they choose to comfort themselves with such statements as, "I couldn't help it," "I've done nothing wrong," "Everybody does it," "It wasn't my fault." These excuses are cold comfort. They are no substitute for the Comforter.

Others try desperately to justify their rebellious actions, preferring to give sophisticated explanations for their self-centred behaviour. This is like the little girl who asked, "Mummy, why is it that when you get irritable you call it nerves and when I get irritable you say it's temper?" We so easily do this. Lust becomes admiration, offence becomes hurt and lies are known as exaggeration. This form of self-justification will never bring true peace and joy.

The upper room gives us a biblical scenario of true and false comfort. Jesus warned His disciples that "one of you will betray me" (John 6:66-71) and "one of you will deny me". He was referring to Judas and Peter. When they had both committed their awful deeds, each sought to find his own comfort.

Judas returned to the priests for solace. Unable to find peace through the money he had earned from his betrayal, he hanged himself (Matthew 27:1-5). He checked out, choosing to annihilate his consciousness of failure and his feelings of guilt. Instead of mourning, and finding comfort in mourning, he extinguished his life.

Peter, on the other hand, was utterly devastated and appalled by what he had done. He "wept bitterly" (Luke 22:61-62). When the Risen Lord appeared to him on the shores of the Sea of Galilee, He cooked breakfast for Peter and then ministered to the deep-seated shame in Peter's life. As Peter felt the tender, restorative grace of his Master, he was grieved. He connected with his sorrow. Instead of suppressing it by going back to fishing, he addressed it and Jesus was delighted with his repentance.

Whereas one man turned to religion and money and found nothing but emptiness, the other turned to God and, through repentance, found true comfort.

Restoring the Power

When my first car wouldn't start in the mornings, as was often the case, a kind member of the church would bring his new car alongside mine and link our batteries by means of a set of starter leads. My powerless battery would then draw from his charged one. In this way, the sufficiency of one made up for the deficiency in the other. That's a picture of what happens when we acknowledge our poverty of spirit and mourn the loss of God's power in our lives. The Holy Spirit draws alongside us, and we are reconnected to God's presence. When that happens, deep comfort fills our souls as God's power is restored.

James, the half-brother of Jesus, said that "God opposes the proud but gives grace to the humble" (James 4:6). What is humility? It is to realize and articulate our complete dependence on God. Pride is the symptom of a heart that has decided to think and act independently from God. Humility is total reliance on God in every area of life. This is why James continues by saying, "Submit yourselves, then, to God. Resist the devil, and he will flee from you. Come near to God and he will come near to you. Wash your hands, you sinners, and purify your hearts, you double-minded. Grieve, mourn and wail. Change your laughter to mourning and your joy to gloom. Humble yourselves before the Lord, and he will lift you up" (James 4:7-10). When we mourn over our spiritual condition, the Comforter comes.

The same promise can also be seen in Paul's words to a church in crisis at Corinth. He begins his second letter by referring to the "God of all comfort", then speaks of his grief over the sexual immorality in the church. Having recognized the penitent brother, he calls for forgiveness and comfort (2 Corinthians 1:3; 2:1-8). "Those who sow in tears will reap with songs of joy" (Psalm 126:5). When we mourn over sin, the joy follows.

The prophet Isaiah takes up the same theme, speaking of an anointing that comes on those who "mourn in Zion" (Isaiah 61:2-3) so as "to grant [consolation and joy] to those who mourn in Zion – to give them an ornament (a garland or diadem) of beauty instead of ashes, the oil of joy for mourning, the garment [expressive] of praise instead of a heavy, burdened, and failing spirit" (Isaiah 61:3, AMP). Those who mourn will rise in the Spirit to "rebuild the ancient ruins", "raise up the former desolations", "renew the ruined cities".

Learning to Look Up

It was a cold winter's morning that welcomed the funeral cortege as it slowly picked its way through the dampened stone epitaphs, the constant reminders of human mortality. Grief-stricken relatives watched as the coffin was lowered into the gaping hole in the ground. The silence of the graveyard was broken only by the voice of an aged cleric dutifully reading the set scriptures and prayers.

As a former serviceman, my departed cousin had been involved in fundraising for various charities. Much time and effort had gone into building his business and aiding various worthy causes. But now his life was over. The remains of someone who had little time for God were about to be laid to rest. The bowed heads and quiet crying just emphasized the sense of hopelessness of a life lived without God.

Family and friends looked longingly into the open grave.

"If only a cure could have been found."

"If only we could have had more time."

But the ravages of cancer had done their worst.

Death seemed so final.

Just then the silence was broken by the sound of a low-flying aircraft. It was approaching at speed. All eyes now turned upwards to the sky. Fingers began to point towards the clouds as a Second World War Spitfire flew low over our heads. In a mark of respect and appreciation for the charitable work done by my cousin, the Royal Air Force had organized this magnificent farewell salute. After flying over our heads once, the pilot returned to perform what is termed the Victory Roll.

The whole scene now changed.

Heads that were bowed now looked up.

Hearts that were dejected now caught a glimmer of hope.

In the heart of human tragedy, there was a reminder of triumph in an enacted display of aeronautical skill.

This is what happens when we mourn as Jesus described it.

This is not the mourning of the bereaved – which is where, to be honest, the story breaks down – but the kind of mourning that characterizes *Life on the Hill*. When we live from heaven's perspective, we cannot be downcast for long. Help is on its way. The comfort is wending its way towards us, performing a victory roll to reassure us that in every trial and tragedy there is the promise of victory.

Make this your angle of approach in life.

Embrace the Be-Attitude of a higher life.

When God seems distant, grieve over what you've lost.

He draws close to the broken-hearted.

Help is on the way.

GROUP DISCUSSION AND PERSONAL APPLICATION GUIDE

Group Discussion:

- Is there a sub-culture of Christianity that says, "This is the day the LORD has made; let us rejoice and be glad in it" (Psalms 118:24) but struggles to embrace a God-inspired "time to mourn" (Ecclesiastes 3:4)?

- When was the last time you grieved the loss of the sense of God's presence and power in your lives?

- Have you ever experienced this dynamic of the comforting presence of God following a period of brokenness?

Personal Application:

- How would you measure yourself on the Spiritual Sensitivity Scale?

- Does your heart break with what breaks God's heart?

- Why not talk to your Spiritual Summiteer about those comforting alternatives you are attached to, rather than finding comfort in God.

When it comes to Personal Application we would encourage you to involve a "Spiritual Summiteer" (see page 37) so as to give yourself some level of accountability and guide you on your upward journey.

BE-ATTITUDE 3

"Blessed are the meek, for they shall inherit the earth."

Meekness is a life submitted to the Master's reins –
strength and passion harnessed to fulfilling
God's will in and through us.

7

DON'T BUCK AUTHORITY

*"He who rules within himself, and rules his passions,
desires and fears, is more than a king."*
John Milton[43]

Twenty metres to the right of where I stood, a young man lowered himself onto the back of an enraged horse. The announcer's voice boomed out of the giant loudspeakers perched on wooden poles in the four corners of the open-air arena. His distinctive North American accent rang out as he outlined the rules of the competition and introduced both cowboy and horse.

The crowd grew quiet. The cowboy would have to stay on the horse for eight seconds holding on with one hand strapped to the saddle. As he prepared himself, he took a deep breath. Then he nodded to those keeping the gated enclosure shut. The chute door swung open. Announcer and crowd started yelling.

The horse exploded out of the gate and began to spin as it kicked and reared its hind legs high in the air, all the time shaking its body to rid itself of the rider. Jerking its head from side to side, the wild animal lurched this way and that across the arena.

The cowboy gripped the horse as tightly as possible, his free hand waving up and down, trying to maintain some semblance of balance. In what followed, there was danger, brute force, flying clods of dirt, a snorting steed, and wildly cheering fans – the rough-and-tumble world of the rodeo.

---

43. John Milton, *Paradise Regained*, (Random House, 2007).

Rodeos, the sport of cowboys, were originally nothing more than an informal gathering of local ranchers during a cattle roundup. They soon developed into an ideal opportunity for farmers to show off their riding skills. One hundred and fifty years ago, most cowboys were young. Young men then, as now, were often less interested in intellectual pursuits than in escapades designed to reveal who was the toughest and fastest.

Their cowboy craft required strength, courage and specific skills. Calves that needed branding did not come when called. They had to be chased down and lassoed. The horses that could catch those calves did not voluntarily give up their freedom for the saddle and bridle. They had to be taught their new role in a hurry; someone had to saddle them, then hang on until the horses accepted their new lifestyle.

The Art of Self-Leadership

Although we may think this kind of unbridled behaviour belongs only to the horses of the Wild West show, it does not. We humans can react to authority in a similar way. How many of us have known people who are a law unto themselves? Independent, isolated, bad-tempered and arrogant, they buck every attempt to restrain them.

Without discipline, none of us can hope to understand, let alone reach, our full potential. Fundamental to all social order is the need for self-control.

Although children may need to be lovingly disciplined to correct their rebellious behaviour, most parents hope that maturity will teach them how to control their waywardness without the need of such correction. The schoolboy who neglects his homework may be detained after school until the work is completed but teachers hope that in time the student in question will learn that self-control brings rewards of freedom of time, the absence of conflict, high marks and better prospects in future life. A young girl may resort to crime; she may steal, destroy, murder or abuse others. The failure to control herself means that others will need to govern her behaviour through penal correction.

Self-control involves governing our motives, attitudes, desires and actions. It is the opposite of what we see in Reuben, an Old Testament character who is described as a man who "boils over". "Reuben, you are my first-born, my might and the beginning (the first fruits) of my manly strength and vigour; [your birth right gave you] the pre-eminence in dignity and the pre-eminence in power. But unstable and boiling over

119

like water you shall not excel and have the pre-eminence [of the first-born] ..." (Genesis 49:3-4, AMP). Although he was pre-eminent in nearly every area of his life, Reuben lacked self-control and therefore forfeited his rights and potential. In the same way, Saul and Solomon lost their right to the throne because they refused to govern themselves.

Joseph, on the other hand, showed fortitude of mind and self-control. Although he was challenged by considerable temptation and the enticement of personal gain, he refused to compromise. Rather than succumb to the seductive advances of Potiphar's wife, he chose to govern his natural desires and escape the temptation (Genesis 39:7-23; 49:23-24).

The results of such self-leadership are not always immediate. Joseph spent time in jail before he could walk into his reward.

But having exercised authority over himself, Joseph was given authority over others. Being put "in charge of the whole land of Egypt ... Pharaoh said to Joseph, 'I am Pharaoh, but without your word no-one will lift hand or foot in all Egypt'" (Genesis 41:41,44). Having first governed himself, Joseph was judged fit to rule others.

You can be the proud owner of a world champion racehorse, but if your prize possession breaks its leg it will be considered worthless. No matter how much a person might glow with potential, a stubborn attitude will render him or her useless. By refusing to accept correction, we forfeit the right to realize our full potential in God. For those who exercise authority, they must first experience authority.

John's Story

John [not his real name] came to our local church, a young man full of promise. The congregation was in desperate need of a pianist; John was musically adept. He seemed to be the answer to a leader's prayer. His measure of musical ability not only included various instruments but also the writing, composing and directing of gospel musicals. He quickly established himself as a very gifted player and was invited to take on the role of chief musician, songwriter and worship leader.

But John had a problem.

He was arrogant, self-willed, independent and unteachable under pressure.

In the months that followed, we recognized John's unique musical gift and wanted to help him reach his full potential. We sought to work alongside him to address these character flaws, but the harder we tried to help him get a grip on his life, the more he bucked the loving and caring authority figures who tried to help. He knew best, and no one was going to tell him how to run his life.

How had John developed these fault lines? An authoritarian father had produced a son with a warped understanding of discipline and authority. To John, rule was restrictive and inconvenient, and therefore a hindrance to his free, creative and artistic spirit. Discipline – so he thought – could never be part of God's training process. If the school of the Spirit included discipleship in its syllabus, he was opting out.

John's "get off my back" attitude became apparent in the church, his marriage and his business career; his spiritual, personal and work life deteriorated to an all-time low. Having made numerous career changes, John's undisciplined attitude proved expensive. This Reuben-type character lost out on all that was potentially his. Eventually, after numerous people tried to help him get a grip on his life and rein himself in, he decided to leave the church. He was now free to roam the wide-open prairies of Christendom, stopping only to drink at charismatic waterholes. He had joined all the other Lone Rangers who exile themselves in a dusty plain of spiritual independence rather than submit to God's rule.

Like the proverbial mule, humanity is born with a stubborn and self-centred nature.

We start life with a rebellious character that needs a radical rebirth if it is to be reined in and harnessed positively. Speaking of those living an uncontrolled lifestyle, the prophet Jeremiah describes them as being like "wild donkeys", showing no measure of personal restraint, running wild, freely venting every natural instinct and exercising little, if any, rule over their wild desires (Jeremiah 2:24-25). Likewise, Isaiah accredits the ox and the donkey with a greater sense of ownership than the rebellious individuals that are hard-hearted towards God's ways (Isaiah 1:2-4). Their unruly nature must be broken; the bit and bridle of godly discipline must be applied if they are to be of any use to the Master. The same is true with an increasingly lawless and anarchic world. External controls may bring people back on the trail for a time, but only divine intervention will ultimately lead to self-leadership.

Meekness is not Weakness

Having set up base camp in the valley of spiritual destitution and having gained a foothold in the cliff face of spiritual mourning, we can now begin our final assault towards the summit where true satisfaction is found, (see page 59). But before we can taste the delights of divine fulness, we must dig deep into the biblical concept of "meekness".

For most English-speaking people, the word "meekness" has negative connotations. Although the original word does not convey this, meekness is often associated with weakness. However, the Bible says, "The man Moses was very meek, above all the men which were upon the face of the earth" (Numbers 12:3, KJV). This same Moses killed an Egyptian; in him, meekness clearly did not equate with weakness.

Commenting on this word, William Barclay wrote, "In our modern English idiom the word meek is hardly one of the honourable words of life. Nowadays it carries with it an idea of spinelessness, and subservience, and mean-spiritedness. It paints the picture of a submissive and ineffective creature. But it so happens that the word meek – in Greek *praus* – was one of the great Greek ethical words."[44]

The easy-going, don't-rock-the-boat, play-it-safe attitude that the world sees as meekness is not the spiritual virtue Jesus is advocating here.

Kingdom meekness is controlled strength. It is an angle of approach to life in which we hold every natural impulse in neutral, ready to respond to the Holy Spirit's prompting.

Meekness is therefore a willing submission to the Master's reins. It is making sure that our character is harnessed and focused towards doing God's will. Christians are charged to show "all meekness unto all men" (Titus 3:2 KJV), to "put on therefore, as the elect of God . . . meekness" (Colossians 3:12, KJV). Meekness is power that has become bridled and therefore full of potential. This idea is contained within the etymological roots of the word *praus. Praus* was used to describe the end-

---

44. William Barclay, *The Daily Study Bible* (St Andrew Press, 1978).

product of the process by which a young colt, wild but full of potential, was harnessed for service. Remember, Jesus rode an untamed colt into Jerusalem. It had never been broken in or bridled, yet it submitted.

Praus, the word Jesus uses, and which is translated "meek", really means "broken in"; it implies great strength, energy and passion harnessed for positive purposes. As it wildly careers over open ground, a colt knows few limitations. For that power to be harnessed, someone must build trust and assert control by teaching it to respond to the rein. By applying pressure to the sensitive areas of its anatomy, the rider teaches the horse to respond to his promptings. Only when a relationship has been established, and the colt submits, is it able to serve its rider. Its strength has not been reduced; it has been channelled towards a positive outcome through a process of discipline.

In similar vein, the virtue known as meekness means exercising control of oneself with the help of the Holy Spirit (Galatians 5:23).

If we are like an unrestrained colt, then the Holy Spirit is like the Horse Whisperer that tames and trains us.

Jesus is therefore not advocating or praising a purely natural ability to control oneself. Such a task is often beyond us in our own strength. It is not natural for us to suppress our emotions, impulses and passions in a purposeful way. No, we need supernatural help in the form of the Holy Spirit. Jesus is commending here the person who is God-controlled, who has learned to recognize and respond to the divine reins of His Word and Spirit. Meekness means:

- Being prepared to take God at His word.

- Letting go of things we stubbornly cling to.

- Refusing to be owned by anything or anyone other than Christ.

- Willingly submitting to Christ's lordship over our lives.

Those who are born again of the Holy Spirit have surrendered their rights as well as given up their wrongs. We can see this illustrated in a telling custom during the Old Testament era. A vendor would take off his sandal and give it to a purchaser to seal the sale and transfer of territory. This was a public declaration of his willingness to surrender his right to walk over the land as the one who had formerly owned it. In the same way, becoming a Christ follower involves an acknowledging of Jesus as Lord, not just accepting Him as Saviour. We voluntarily hand over all personal rights and invite the new owner to do with us as He sees fit. In short, we take off our sandals.

Meekness is accordingly an angle of approach to life in which we maintain a willingness and openness for God to break and rein us in whenever this is needed. A bridle is for restraint, control and direction; through it, the horse knows its master's will. Its use will cause an animal eventually to yield its strength and thus reach its full potential.

Taking Your Self to the Gym

We, too, are in training. When Paul told Timothy to train himself to be godly (1 Timothy 4:7; 2 Timothy 2:1-5; 3:10-17), he used a Greek word from which we get "gymnastics". He was literally saying, "engage in the gymnastics of the self" and "sharpen and develop your character and ministry through the disciplined application of biblical truth".

Disciples are learners more than mere students. They are committed to the person doing the teaching. When John the Baptist's disciples fasted, their conduct reflected the kind of man John was. The Pharisees reproduced followers "twice as much a son of hell" as themselves (Matthew 23:15). As Jesus called people to follow Him, He stated the personal commitment required: "Walk with me and work with me – watch how I do it. Learn the unforced rhythms of grace" (Matthew 11:29, MSG). In commissioning His first followers, Jesus said that the essence of making disciples is "teaching them to observe" (Matthew 28:18-20, ESV).

By building a loving and trusting relationship with His followers, Jesus's style of teaching was more living room than classroom.

While the classroom model is upfront, verbal, academic, the living room is more relational, experiential, assessed and accountable, an apprenticeship style of learning. While the academic approach produces students paying lip-service to the subject, the apprentice approach of Jesus produces a change of lifestyle. This is because the Jesus way includes both a lesson we listen to and a lifestyle we observe

Only a loving, nurturing and secure environment can hope to encourage changes in people's lives. The ill-treatment that life often deals out can create a void of suspicion, hesitancy, uncertainty and mistrust. This creates a gulf that needs to be bridged if we are to listen to the advice and counsel of others.

Gentle Training
When taking up the role of house parents in a new children's home, some friends of mine decided to buy a horse. After first

trading in an old, bedraggled donkey, they managed to buy a fine pedigree pony. The animal went by the name of "Fireball XL Five" and showed great promise. It looked ideal to use for riding lessons, but first the animal needed to be trained. Because of previous ill-treatment, the animal was wild.

After a great deal of time and effort, the weeks of being handfed and receiving kindness began to pay off. At last they were able to get the pony to accept a bit and bridle and then eventually a saddle. Sadly, that was as far as the training process ever got. The patience of the staff was not shared by the children. During a spell when the house parents were away from the home, one of the children decided to speed up the training programme by using a pool cue across the creature's flanks. As a result, the pony reverted to its old ways and never regained its trust in anyone from that home.

Meekness is an angle of approach to life whereby we welcome the dealings of God and trusted people with no fear of abuse or aggression. We submit to the gentle discipline of our loving heavenly Father. Living under God's control, we act with self-control. We allow the dealings of God to restrain and redirect our energies into "good works, which God prepared beforehand, that we should walk in them" (Ephesians 2:10, ESV).

When he was opposed by Miriam and Aaron, Moses – a man noted for his meekness – did not retaliate. Instead, as is so often seen in this man's life, his approach was to allow God's dealings to control and direct things. Jesus similarly epitomized this attitude. "When they hurled their insults at him, he did not retaliate; when he suffered, he made no threats. Instead, he entrusted himself to him who judges justly" (1 Peter 2:23). This is so counter-intuitive for human beings.

How often, when faced with God's pull of adjustment in our lives, do we want to buck authority?

We should submit to the Father's gentle training, knowing that His loving discipline brings a harvest of righteousness.

Possessing the Earth

We live in an age where freedom and authority are viewed as opposites. Those who advocate discipline are viewed as diametrically opposed to those who express a free spirit. The values of our forefathers are regarded as archaic and irrelevant. The idea of any hierarchy within what was once called the nuclear family is refuted. A gauntlet has been thrown down before historic human values. The right to self-rule is championed. People cry out for equal rights, human rights, workers' rights, and women's rights. One big question faces our culture: "Authority – who has it and who dares to exercise it?"

In this world, the Church must emerge as salt and light and be at the forefront of the argument about authority. If the Church abstains from the debate because of indifference, isolation or ignorance, it will create a moral vacuum and humanity will self-destruct. Society needs no more thermometers, monitoring the ups and downs of our present social climate. It needs thermostats which will regulate the moral temperature of the nation. Such is the God-given role of the Church.

It is said that when Horatio Nelson found two officers arguing on the deck of his ship moments before the Battle of Trafalgar, he pointed to the French fleet on the horizon and said, "Gentlemen, there's your enemy."

Meekness is that God-given ability to harness our impulses in a positive and right direction.

Meekness becomes controlled strength; it is directed against the real enemy rather than against each other.

Very few modern thinkers would ever consider, let alone propound, meekness as a vital ingredient for success. Yet Jesus saw meekness as a key component to becoming a winner. "Blessed are the meek, for they will inherit the earth" (Matthew 5:5, paraphrased). Carl Sanburg described Abraham Lincoln as "a man of steel and velvet". Mark van Doren says, "To me, Lincoln seems, in some ways, the most interesting man who ever lived. He was gentle, but this gentleness was combined with a terrific toughness, an iron strength."[45] Those are the two sides of meekness, right there! And there is a reward for exhibiting this kind of meekness in our lives. The promise of "inheriting the earth" is said to derive from Psalm 37 verse 11: "The meek will inherit the land and enjoy great peace." The psalm describes a people who are not able to overcome the power of the wicked and need therefore to rely on God. They in turn are promised that God will establish them in such a way as to inherit what is rightfully theirs – the land.

"The earth is the LORD's and everything in it," says Psalm 24:1. God promised the people of Israel that they would possess the land of Canaan (Leviticus 20:24). This foreshadowed God's promise of the earth to the people of faith (Romans 4:13). Here, then, is a crucial attitude for those who want to be involved in advancing God's kingdom on earth – meekness. Since this promise involves the earth, we must guard against becoming so parochial that we fail to possess the totality of what God has planned.

Many today speak as if the Church is engaged in a kind of Custer's-last-stand.

---

45. Aubrey Andelin, *Man of Steel and Velvet* (Bantam Books, 1983).

Christians are portrayed as a minority waiting for the second coming of Jesus as if it were the arrival of God's cavalry with trumpets blasting and sabres glistening. Yet Paul, writing to the church at Ephesus, reminds us that Christ will come for "a radiant church, without stain or wrinkle or any other blemish, but holy and blameless" (Ephesians 5:27).

God's purpose remains unchanged from the beginning. He commanded men and women to "be fruitful and increase in number; fill the earth and subdue it" (Genesis 1:28). Our task is to work with God so that His kingdom will come as His will is done. And meekness is fundamental to our success.

Your Will be Done!

A man may have the desire to line up his will with God's but, as much as he tries, he cannot do it in his own strength: "For what I want to do I do not do, but what I hate I do" (Romans 7:15). Like an unbroken horse, the human will, motivated by its natural instincts, stubbornly pursues a course of action with little thought for the consequences. It resists all attempts by external influences to redirect its path; it is doing what comes naturally. Like the proverbial donkey, the will is strong, stubborn and selfish.

In contrast, God's will is perfectly expressed by Jesus who could say, "I always do what pleases [the Father]" (John 8:29). At the same time, the Bible says that "'although he was a son, he learned obedience from what he suffered" (Hebrews 5:8, ESV). Jesus's success in always doing the Father's will came out of a learning process that included the personal inconvenience and pain of rejecting temptation and obeying God. As we seek to harness our will to do God's will, we find in Christ a perfect example to follow.

Without the redemptive work of the Holy Spirit, the will of the unregenerate person is primed to self-destruct.

In other words, we are a people who "die for lack of discipline" (Proverbs 5:23). Only through the miracle of new birth can human beings become "a new creation" in which "the old has gone, the new has come" (2 Corinthians 5:17). Therefore, as "participators in the divine nature", the regenerate man takes control of every natural desire and, reflecting the nature of Christ, submits to God's purposes, praying, "Father . . . not as I will, but as you will" (Matthew 26:39). Meekness is therefore not weakness. Nor is it being belligerent, fighting for what we want. True meekness has a serving attitude and a willingness to submit to authority, to allow the dealings of God and people in our lives without retaliation. It is not bucking authority, nor is it reacting by crying out, "Get off my back!"

Aubrey Andelin writes, "The foundation of a noble character is self-mastery. It is the key to applying any virtue in which we may be lacking and will carry us to our greatest objective – becoming a perfect individual. Self-mastery is the means whereby we apply knowledge of basic principles, overcome weakness, conquer appetites and passions, and devote ourselves to duty and reach our objectives . . . Self-mastery is the motivating force whereby we reach upward."[46]

Those who want to exercise authority must be under authority. They must be under God's authority and, at the same time, exercise self-leadership.

Alexander the Great, one of history's most famous motivators, led his army of thousands across desert and mountain. Yet his ability to lead became somewhat compromised when, in a

---

46. Aubrey Andelin, *Man of Steel and Velvet* (Bantam Books, 1983).

drunken stupor, he lost his temper and in the ensuing brawl speared his friend Cleitus to death.

To take control, I must be under control.

Kingdom rule must begin in me before it can extend to others.

It's time to learn meekness.

GROUP DISCUSSION AND
PERSONAL APPLICATION GUIDE

Group Discussion:

- Does anyone have any scary horse-riding stories?

- Although we all like to see meekness in the Mother Teresas and Nelson Mandelas of this world, to advocate meekness in us can be a different matter. Discuss.

- Can a negative view of authority be based on a bad experience? If so, how do we overcome this?

Personal Application:

- How often, when faced with God's pull towards adjustment in our lives, do you want to buck authority?

- Have your past experiences, education or environment coloured your thinking on godly authority? If so, is this something you would like to speak to your "Spiritual Summiteer" about?

When it comes to Personal Application we would encourage you to involve a "Spiritual Summiteer" (see page 37) so as to give yourself some level of accountability and guide you on your ongoing journey.

BE-ATTITUDE 4

"Blessed are those who hunger and thirst for righteousness, for they will be filled."

Maintaining a healthy appetite for rightness with God that causes us to spill Jesus everywhere we go.

8

LAST SEEN HEADING FOR THE TOP

"The secret of spiritual success is a hunger that persists. It is an awful condition to be satisfied with one's spiritual attainment. God was and is looking for hungry, thirsty, desperate people."
Smith Wigglesworth[47]

For those suffering from "summit fever" – that compelling desire to reach the top of a mountain at all costs – your patience is about to be rewarded; the peak of all that Jesus taught concerning attitudes is now within our reach!

Jesus said, "You're blessed when you've worked up a good appetite for God. He's food and drink in the best meal you'll ever eat" (Matthew 5:6, MSG). With these words, we are only moments away from the pinnacle of all that has gone before, (see page 59). Having an intense hunger for God is the highest aspiration for all Christ followers. A Christ follower is someone who knows that true satisfaction is only found in God. Spiritual hunger is therefore essential. It is a way of life for the one who loves Jesus. It is also essential in the life of every seeker. Only those who are spiritually hungry will find God.

If we do not grasp this, then our reading of the Be-Attitudes will be nothing more than a rerun of "The Grand Old Duke of York".

---

47. Dr Michael H. Yeager, *The Miracle of Smith Wigglesworth* (Copyright © 2015 Dr Michael H. Yeager).

It will be a formulaic and futile march to the top of the hill and then down again. Without spiritual destitution, mourning, meekness and hunger – deep, desperate hunger – we will never live *Life on the Hill*, let alone engage and conquer the enemy. Maintaining our hunger for God is not only a prerequisite for discipleship; it is the vital precondition for social transformation.

The View from the Top!

In a short public life that lasted only twelve years, Martin Luther King Jr managed to change the course of history. As a hero of the civil rights movement, he championed a cause that was to transform America. Advocating a non-violent approach to public protest, he became one of America's leading lights during the dark days of segregation. With the eloquence of a master orator, he holds a revered and unparalleled place in Black American history.

On the evening of 3rd April 1968, King spoke to a strike rally in Memphis. It was here that he delivered his famous "I've been to the mountaintop" speech. "We have been forced to a point where we're going to have to grapple with the problems that men have been trying to grapple with through history," he said, "but the demands didn't force them to do it. Survival demands that we grapple with them. Men, for years now, have been talking about war and peace. But now no longer can they just talk about it. It is no longer a choice between violence and non-violence in this world; it's non-violence or non-existence..."

With that, Dr King issued his rallying cry. "Let us rise up tonight with a greater readiness. Let us stand with a greater determination. And let us move on in these powerful days, these days of challenge, to make America a better nation. And

I want to thank God, once more, for allowing me to be here with you ..."

At this point, Dr King moved to prophecy. He shared a dream that he had been given – a dream that he knew came from the heart of God. "I don't know what will happen now. We've got some difficult days ahead. But it doesn't matter with me now, because I've been to the mountaintop. And I don't mind. Like anybody, I would like to live a long life; longevity has its place. But I'm not concerned about that now. I just want to do God's will. And He's allowed me to go up to the mountain. And I've looked over. And I've seen the Promised Land. I may not get there with you. But I want you to know tonight that we as a people will get to the Promised Land. And I'm happy tonight, I'm not worried about anything. I'm not fearing any man. Mine eyes have seen the glory of the coming of the Lord."[48]

The following evening, on his way to a friend's house for dinner, Dr King paused on the balcony outside his motel to talk to staff members. Suddenly, without warning, an assassin's bullet hit him. Moments later, the visionary was dead. Like Moses – whose life he references in this memorable speech – Dr King had been to the top of his mountain. He had caught a glimpse of a Promised Land where "the sons of former slaves and the sons of former slave owners will be able to sit down together at the table of brotherhood".

It was a land where injustice and oppression would give way to freedom and justice; where human beings would not be judged by the colour of their skin, but by the content of their character.

---

48. Coretta Scott King, *The Words of Martin Luther King, Jr.* (HarperCollins, 2001).

What is the greatest speech ever given? Most people would answer, "The Sermon on the Mount, followed by Dr King's speech." Dr King dreamed of a mountain summit, a vantage point from which he saw a future of racial equality. Jesus had a dream too, a dream shared on a mountain top, a dream in which his followers all over the world would embrace some Be-Attitudes, attitudes that would transform their love for God and their love for their neighbour. While Dr King's dream spoke to the heart, Jesus's sermon speaks to the spiritual component of our being. In this respect, being spiritually hungry for God needs to precede being politically motivated. Only those who have ascended the hill of the Lord and become thoroughly overwhelmed by the presence and purpose of God are adequately prepared to confront the injustice and oppression in today's world. If the local church really is the hope for the world, then Christ followers can only be agents of lasting change if they are totally reliant on God, rather than dependent on their own ideas and resources.

This is why the first four Be-Attitudes (which deal with our *relying* on God) need to precede the second four (which deal with our *relating* with others). Having begun on the nursery slopes of spiritual poverty, plotted a course through the challenging terrain of mourning, and successfully traversed the steep learning curve of biblical meekness, we are ready for the final push towards the summit – the place towards which our holy desperation is driving us, the place where true satisfaction is found.

While we pause here, we must understand that spiritual hunger is not a place to visit but a place to reside. Only by maintaining our spiritual hunger will we remain close to God. In intimate relationship with Him, we will then find the solutions to the world's problems. The blueprints for bringing heaven to earth are at the summit, in His presence. When we experience His mercy, we can show mercy to others. When we enjoy His peace, we can be peacemakers in places of conflict. The key is to keep on being hungry for the presence of God, where we find our true satisfaction.

Righteousness Revisited

At this point, it is important that we take a fresh look at a complicated biblical word, "righteousness". Righteousness means being in a right relationship with a righteous God. The only way this can happen is if a person confesses where they have gone wrong (both in their attitudes and actions) and then comes to believe and confess that Jesus Christ is their Lord and Saviour. In other words, when people repent of sin and then believe that Jesus Christ has paid the full price for sin at Calvary, then they are right with God. Those who believe in the finished work of the cross are accordingly righteous people. They live in a right relationship with God not because of what they have done but solely because of what Jesus has done.

It is important at this point to realize that this critical moment, when a person admits they have been in the wrong but believes that Jesus alone has put it right, does two very precious things. Using the language of the courtroom is helpful here. Firstly, this critical moment means that God declares us "not guilty!" In other words, in His eyes, we are no longer in the wrong. Secondly, this same moment secures another great blessing. God declares that we are "in the right", thanks to what His Son has achieved on the cross. These are the two great blessings of justification. As Dr Billy Graham used to say, "When we are justified, it is just-as-if-I'd-never-sinned."

This first understanding we might call "legal righteousness".

But there is more to Biblical righteousness than this. There is secondly what we might call "ethical righteousness". A quick glance at the Sermon on the Mount will reveal that Jesus was not only interested in helping us to live in a right relationship with God. He was also intentional about inspiring us to put right the wrongs of this fallen and corrupt world. In order for Christ followers to do that, they must embrace the Be-Attitudes of the Sermon on the Mount. They must embrace the kingdom attitudes that are essential for living in a right relationship with God, but they then need to embrace the kingdom attitudes that are essential for resolving the wrongs of this world, and particularly for restoring the rights of those who are wronged by the world's oppressive social systems. The righteousness of God is by its very nature relational and involves being and doing right. If it is not social in its outworking, it is not true godly righteousness, because:

"Social involvement [is] both the child of evangelical religion and the twin sister of evangelism."[49]

---

49. John Stott, *Involvement: Being a Responsible Christian in a Non-Christian Society* (Word, 1985).

What we need, therefore, is a BOTH-AND theology – BOTH *legal* righteousness (being in a right relationship with God) AND *social* righteousness (putting right the wrongs of this world). Unless we fully understand our position of being right before God, we will wallow in the mud of insecurity and live isolated lives. Unless we realize that righteousness also means social reform, the Church will never be heard in the debates about social injustice and human oppression. Each believer must therefore maintain his or her appetite for righteousness. As Jesus said, "Seek first his kingdom and his righteousness, and all these things will be given to you as well" (Matthew 6:33).

All this means we must learn how to reside in a kingdom whose roots are righteousness and whose fruit is the transformation of human relationships through the power of the Holy Spirit. When we hunger and thirst for true righteousness, God not only does a great work *in* us, He also begins to do a great work *through* us. Spiritual hunger is therefore a vital and foundational virtue of living *Life on the Hill*.

Staying Hungry for Righteousness

Perhaps you are realizing now how important it is not only to be hungry for God's righteousness before we are saved, but for our whole lives. *Saving righteousness* must, in short, lead to *social righteousness*. Jesus develops this theme by addressing thinking, speaking and relating to others in a right way.

1) THINKING RIGHTLY (Matthew 5:27-30)
We live in a promiscuous society in which any kind of sexual perversion seems not only to be acceptable but desirable.

Living under the sovereignty of God means hungering and thirsting for moral purity.

It means not entertaining lustful thoughts and uncontrolled desires – the renegade passions that cause us to covet others, to reach out and touch, to take or taste what is not rightfully ours. Such desires must be corralled and controlled with the bit and bridle of godly discipline. As Jesus says, "If your right eye causes you to sin, gouge it out and throw it away . . . And if your right hand causes you to sin, cut it off and throw it away" (Matthew 5:29-30). This is an instance of hyperbole. Jesus is making a point by deliberate exaggeration. If every Christ follower took this saying literally, there would be millions of one-eyed musicians trying to play the keyboard or guitar with only one hand. No, Jesus is indicating that a radical problem requires a radical remedy. If your addiction is alcohol, don't look at adverts for alcoholic drinks, and don't grab the free glass of champagne at that wedding reception. Turn the TV off when the advert comes on and reach out for the glass of orange juice when the silver tray is proffered to you. Radical steps are needed because the alternative is deadly – the destruction of the human soul.[50]

2) SPEAKING RIGHTLY (Matthew 5:33-37)

Jesus encourages His followers to maintain an appetite for verbal honesty and godly conversations. This means "[making] sure it's all gone for good: bad temper, irritability, meanness, profanity, dirty talk. Don't lie to one another. You're done with that old life. It's like a filthy set of ill-fitting clothes you've stripped off and put in the fire" (Colossians 3:8-9, MSG). To repeat my wife's mantra, "If you cannot say anything nice, don't say anything at all." Speaking rightly also means avoiding the temptation to exaggerate to impress others, or to be manipulative to persuade others. It means being constructive,

---

50. Many people find that in support groups like Celebrate Recovery, Weight Watchers, Alcoholics Anonymous, etc., they are able to find mutual help! Righteousness is relational so with God and friends it is easier to stay on track.

not destructive, open and honest in speaking with others. It means ensuring that our word is our bond.

Words carry the potential for both good and evil, life and death.

You can become "ensnared by the words of your mouth" (Proverbs 6:2, NASB). And because the Lord knows our words before they are spoken, our prayer should be, "Set a guard over my mouth, O LORD . . . [so that] the words of my mouth and the meditation of my heart [may be] pleasing" to the Lord (Psalm 141:3, Psalm 19:14).

3) RELATING RIGHTLY (Matthew 5:21-26; 18:15)

Much of the Sermon on the Mount describes how we are to relate in a right way towards other people. In fact, Jesus's teaching here gets right down to brass tacks, dealing in a practical way with what He expects our relationships to look like. Take anger for example. Anger is not necessarily always wrong. God gets angry but He does not sin in His anger. Righteous anger therefore has its place. We sin when we get angry without a justified reason. As Jesus said, "Whosoever is angry with his brother *without a cause* shall be in danger of the judgment" (Matthew 5:22, KJV). In Ephesians 4:26-27, Paul taught, "In your anger do not sin." He added, "Do not let the sun go down while you are still angry, and do not give the devil a foothold." In other words, there is an anger that is righteous – an anger that seeks to address the wrongs of this world as God sees them. But there is also an unrighteous anger – a rage towards others that is not founded in God's grief over the world's wrongs but over the frustration of our own self-interests and egotistical goals. The question we must always ask is this:

"Is my anger rooted in a just and righteous cause? Or am I reacting because my personal feelings, pride or prejudices have been affected?" We must let the indwelling Spirit of God judge our motives. Our desire to protect covenantal relationships (such as marriage) must give us an added motivation to put things right. Covenantal loyalty[51] demands that I do all I can to bring a resolve to the issue at hand (Romans 12:18-19).

Where I have offended someone, or they have offended me, the responsibility to resolve the conflict is always mine.

"Therefore if . . . your brother has something against you . . . go and be reconciled to your brother" (Matthew 5:23-24). "If your brother sins against you, go and show him his fault, just between the two of you" (Matthew 18:15). The sad fact is that too many believers do not apply these principles. We attempt to worship together without resolving our differences. Maintaining a healthy spiritual appetite requires that we think rightly, speak rightly and relate rightly. Saving righteousness without social righteousness is quite simply wrong.

Appetite Spoilers

The Bible teaches us that "righteousness exalts a nation" (Proverbs 14:34). The heroes of this generation will therefore have a "righteousness consciousness". They will not only make

---

51. *Covenantal Loyalty* – although not a part of everyday Christian conversation, the word *"Covenant"* is crucial to our understanding God's dealings with His people. A covenant is a *binding agreement*. Through faith in the redemptive work of Christ, God the Father wants to initiate a loving, loyal and lasting relationship with humanity. *Covenantal Loyalty* is illustrated in God's view of marriage as a life-long commitment, a "binding agreement", a loving relationship that works out, rather than walks away from our differences.

sure that they remain hungry for a right relationship with their loving heavenly Father (legal righteousness), they will also ensure that they maintain a healthy appetite for living in a right relationship with other people (social righteousness). They will develop a working knowledge of what it means to *be* right with God and what it means to *act* rightly for others. As committed guardians of God's righteousness, they will avoid those appetite spoilers that the apostle Peter warns us of in 1 Peter 2:1-3, such as:

- Malice – deliberately wanting to hurt others.
- Deceit – twisting the truth.
- Hypocrisy – being two-faced.
- Envy – jealous of others.
- Slander – talking destructively behind someone's back.

What if I lack any interest in spiritual things? I would simply say the following in response.

The way to regain your spiritual appetite is by firstly retracing the steps that have brought you here.

Trek back to base camp and exchange your independent attitude for a renewed dependence on God, a revitalized interdependence with those you trust. Next, allow the Holy Spirit to soften your heart so that you become sensitive to those things that grieve God. The final step for this work of restoration is to invite your heavenly Father to pick up the reins and direct your life, as He alone sees fit.

Intense Hunger and Thirst

Just as in the natural part of our lives our appetite is a basic means of sustaining life and growth, so it is in the spiritual realm. When we lack spiritual hunger and thirst, this is often a sign of a spiritual disorder which, left unchecked, will prove disastrous. To hunger and thirst for righteousness is to demonstrate a deep desire for all that God has for us.

The problem is that most Westerners have little experience of real hunger and thirst, so our frame of reference is somewhat limited. When was the last time we experienced long, sustained hunger or thirst for food or water? For the comfortable and consumerist West, where there are fast-food outlets everywhere, these metaphors of hungering and thirsting do not immediately strike us with force. However, the Holy Spirit can enable us to know *supernaturally* that which surpasses knowledge *naturally* (Ephesians 3:19).

When Jesus spoke of hungering and thirsting, He chooses His words carefully. The normal Greek word for hunger and thirst would indicate a low-level desire for a piece of bread or a glass of water. But the word used here implies "an intense hunger and thirst for all that is available". This is no mild appetite – a feeling of being peckish for some spiritual snack. This is an aching hunger and a raging thirst for God. Arthur Wallis makes the distinction well. He writes, "Hunger is a cry from the whole body stemming from need. We might say, then, that mere appetite relates to the immediate 'want' of the stomach, true hunger to the real 'need' of the body."[52]

When the prodigal son began to be "in need", he turned to the pig swill. When he was "starving", he returned to his father.

---

52. Arthur Wallis, *God's Chosen Fast* (CLC, 2015).

This Be-Attitude is therefore no momentary desire, no passing fancy or whim. It is a deep need affecting our whole being, an intense hunger and thirst for all that is available in Christ Jesus.

We can see a picture of this more intense expression of hunger and thirst in the Old Testament story about a famine that struck Samaria. The lepers who risked everything to find food teach us some vital keys to true hunger and thirst. Deep hunger and thirst proved to be powerful motivators for these men. Their desperation caused them to be reckless. In the same way, a spiritual hunger will do the following:

- Focus our vision.
- Get rid of the unnecessary. Many people will remember the harrowing reports on TV of families making mammoth journeys to escape famine, their belongings left beside the road. Things once thought vital to life now become secondary and unimportant.

A true spiritual thirst for God will not only crystallize our vision. It will cause us to shed those things we once eagerly sought.

- Sharpen our desires.
- Motivate us to move out of mediocrity.
- Make us radical risktakers.
- Cause us to speak up and speak out.

Spiritual hunger of this kind will result in us knowing the satisfaction for which humanity longs. As one wise observer said about our appetite for food, "Without a healthy appetite, mealtimes become a drudgery instead of a delight." The same is true in the spiritual realm. Without maintaining a strong spiritual appetite for all things godly, spiritual disciplines will become a laborious chore.

Lots of Leftovers

Jesus said, "I came that they may have and enjoy life, and have it in abundance (to the full, till it overflows)" (John 10:10, AMP). Some people give a casual nod to this promise while others give it a whoop of joy. Both are sometimes evidence of a superficial knowledge of what Jesus is saying. Those who cultivate a deep desire and a holy longing for living in a right relationship with God, and with one's neighbour, will know experientially what Jesus meant. They will be completely satisfied and filled, living life in all its super-abundance, filled to the brim and overflowing to others.

When Jesus fed the four thousand, we are told "they ate and were satisfied" (Mark 8:8). Afterwards, they picked up seven basketfuls of that "which was left over". The people were satisfied, and there was plenty to spare. The same happens in the feeding of the 5,000 in Luke's gospel (Luke 9:12-17). Here the seed for the miracle was a lad's willingness to give up his meagre lunch. Once this packed lunch was blessed by Jesus, everyone enjoyed fullness, satisfaction and contentment in an abundance of loaves and fishes.

In Christ, we can tap into a divine source of supply that will not only meet our immediate needs but the needs of others. A super-abundant life means having enough to meet my needs and more besides. It means enjoying an overflow of energy, time, finance, ability and resource to meet the needs of others. This is why the apostle Paul states, "Your abundance at the present time should supply their need" (2 Corinthians 8:13-14, ESV). In God's kingdom economy, the measure He metes out is fullness. Put another way, it is a "good measure, pressed down, shaken together and running over" (Luke 6:38).

Finding and maintaining this level of fullness is what will cause Christians to break free of their ghetto mentality to minister out of fullness to those in need within their sphere of influence.

How crucial it us for us to experience fullness before we begin relating to people! Only a person who knows mercy can show mercy. Only those who have experienced God's peace can make peace. Only if we have been made pure within can we hope to serve others from a pure motive. It is through this divine measure of fullness that we will overflow with the life and love of God in our relationship with others.

Two Hands

Being a house-proud father with four growing children was at times challenging. The balance between an ordered or organic style of parenting was for me a constant battle, especially in matters of food and drink. Let me put it out there: I hate handling kids with sticky fingers! There, I've said it! On the rare occasions we could afford to eat out, I feared a meltdown by an impetuous child that would end up as a public food fight, much to the embarrassment of other customers. These fears were no less strong in the privacy of our home. The possibility of staining our antique furniture made me nervous. When handing a drink to any of our four children, my request was always the same, despite there being a twelve-year age difference between them. Whether it was a cup, mug or plastic tumbler, drinks were always filled to the brim. So, whenever I handed out drinks, the gesture would always be accompanied by the words, "Two hands, please!" My reasoning was that gripping the container with both hands was more likely to reduce the likelihood of accidents. The problem was that I had put "spillage" in the minds of my children, leading to my fears being fulfilled!

Many years on, I am now experiencing a reverse-psychology. Whenever my adult children hand a drink to me, their ageing father, they will often accompany this with the words, "Two hands, Dad. Two hands, please!"

The truth is, when it comes to living *Life on the Hill*, we are called to do two things. We are firstly encouraged to take hold of what satisfies us spiritually with both hands, and to take our fill of that. Secondly, we are urged to let the goodness of what has satisfied us overflow to others, so that they in turn may be satisfied.

In the Kingdom of Heaven, therefore, God is not a Father who is fearful of us spilling what He has given us. He actively invites us to be spillers. And He delights when others get splashed in the overflow of what He's given us!

This, then, is a far more joyful vision of generosity. In more legalistic settings of the Church, preachers tell their flock to serve others and witness to non-believers. All this becomes a form of guilt-edged religion in which we try to do these things in our own strength, but then fail miserably, and find ourselves miserable over our failures. How much better it is to draw on God's resources and to be so filled with the Father's love that we cannot resist giving it away to others! How much more joyful it is to speak with our mouths out of the abundance that the Father has poured into our hearts.

This is not guilt-edged religion; it is grace-based relationship. It is evangelism that is supernaturally natural!

The importance of spiritual fullness cannot therefore be overstated. This is why, after He had taught the disciples for forty days about the Kingdom of God, the Risen Jesus told His followers to remain in Jerusalem until they were enveloped in power. This was vital; the disciples were vulnerable and afraid. But once they were endued with power from on high, they were able to overflow with the love of God to others.

Maintaining a state of fullness and fulfilment is therefore vital. You cannot visit the source of true satisfaction on an infrequent basis. You need to go on being filled. This is *Life on the Hill*, a lifestyle motivated by a thirst for spiritual abundance. We cannot minister to a fractured world out of the residue of some past spiritual blessing. As the great evangelist D.L. Moody once said, "We are leaky vessels and must continually be refilled."

An artesian well is a miracle of nature. It does not require a pump to bring fresh water to the surface. It naturally and continually overflows. This may be an oversimplification, but maybe the lack of enthusiasm to share our story of faith with others is because we are trying, through human effort, to pump from a dry well. The abundant life Jesus promises us, living a life with more than enough left over for others, will cause us to find ourselves spilling Jesus everywhere we go.

When that happens, our heavenly Father will not chastise us. He will rejoice over us with singing (Zephaniah 3:17).

GROUP DISCUSSION AND PERSONAL APPLICATION GUIDE

Group Discussion:

- What smell is guaranteed to trigger your appetite?
- Can you think of anyone whose appetite for God has left a lasting legacy that would earn them the epitaph: *'Last seen heading for the top?*
- What adjustments do you need to make in thinking rightly, speaking rightly and relating rightly to others?
- What are your thoughts on "spilling Jesus" into our home, office, school, church, family, friends and society at large?

Personal Application:

- How is your spiritual appetite? Along with a "Spiritual Sherpa", do you need to talk about "Appetite Spoilers" and maybe retrace your steps and revisit Be-Attitudes 1–3, asking God to restore your hunger and thirst for spiritual things?
- Is what you are spilling in your home, church or workplace, positive or negative?

When it comes to Personal Application we would encourage you to involve a "Spiritual Summiteer" (see page 37) so as to give yourself some level of accountability and guide you on your ongoing journey.

IT'S TIME TO SHINE!

*"Not all of us can do great things.
But we can do small things with great love."*

Mother Teresa

BE-ATTITUDE 5

"Blessed are the merciful, for they will be shown mercy."

The ability to empathize with others in order to exercise heavenly justice not earthly judgment.

9

STRANGERS ON A TRAIN

"You never really understand a person until . . .
you climb inside of his skin and walk around in it."
Harper Lee, *To Kill a Mockingbird*[53]

Visitors looking for an authentic London experience almost always try riding the London Underground. However, if this is something high up on their bucket list, they should be aware; Londoners who have spent much of their lives negotiating the network have an Underground etiquette that is second nature to them. For the uninitiated, the perils of taking the Tube can be overwhelming, especially during rush hour. Squeezed together with strangers like proverbial sardines can be daunting. Confronted by a kaleidoscope of humanity and surrounded by a cacophony of sounds, riding the underground is not as much fun as the term might suggest. Thrown into a melting-pot of people from a mix of social backgrounds, travellers and tourists find themselves in a carriage with characters that would not look out of place in crime thrillers, comedy capers, Rom Coms and horror stories.

Travelling late one Sunday night, one Londoner was hoping for a relaxing ride home. Having spent a busy day attending various inner-city churches, this weary vicar was peopled out. As his mind drifted off, he found time to reflect on his superb sermon, "Getting Down off Your High Horse". He had spoken about the Good Samaritan in Luke's gospel. With his carefully

---

53. Harper Lee, *To Kill a Mockingbird* (first published in Great Britain by William Heinemann, 1960; Arrow Books, 2010).

crafted words, the vicar had eloquently pleaded for his listeners to see people beaten up by life as an opportunity to serve, not an obstacle to avoid.

Smug with his expository brilliance, the vicar was now enjoying an undisturbed journey home.

Avoiding eye-contact with his fellow passengers, he occasionally looked up at the map to check where he was on the District Line. The next station was Paddington. When the train arrived, the brightly lit platform was dotted with only a few passengers. Hoping this meant that his journey would continue undisturbed, the vicar noticed a trio of figures waiting near the doors to his carriage. A father, and what appeared to be his two sons, looked hassled and distraught. The dad was trying his best to hold on to his irritated children and was visibly relieved when eventually the doors opened, whereupon he released his brood on the poor, unsuspecting passengers.

On entering the near-empty carriage, the two well-dressed but ill-behaved children set about causing mayhem. Treating the train like a theme-park ride, they ran the full length of the carriage, jumping on and off seats and swinging from the handrails like creatures in a zoo. All the while, the father did nothing.

By now, the vicar was feeling a mixture of anger and superiority, thanking God that his children would never behave like this. "Why does this father not get a grip of his kids?" Analysing the scene with the expertise of a family liaison officer and a celebrated psychologist, he concluded that this was a classic case of two children trying to attract the attention of an emotionally distant dad.

Eventually, the decibels and disturbance subsided as the father calmly asked his boys to settle down.

"Settle down!" the vicar thought. "What they need is some firm parental discipline!"

The vicar was the nearest passenger to the beleaguered dad, whose shoulders drooped under the heavy burden. Leaning forward, the father started to engage in conversation with the vicar. As he began to speak, the vicar noticed that the man's face was ashen and his eyes bloodshot. This did little to change his judgmental view.

The father muttered a few unintelligible words that sounded like, "I'm so sorry."

"Sorry!" thought the self-righteous vicar. "Sorry does not begin to compensate for what your two children have been up to!"

Attempting a wry smile, the vicar averted his eyes.

Realizing his simple sorry was not enough, the father spoke again. "I'm so sorry, sir, for my children's behaviour. We have just come from the hospital. The boys have just said goodbye to their mother. We're all finding it difficult handling our grief."

Feeling ashamed, the vicar tried his best to redeem himself. He offered a sympathetic smile along with some words of comfort.

But it was too late.

The words sounded empty.

No matter what he said, nothing could make up for his absence of Christian charity. How hollow his sermon now seemed! If only he had embraced a different angle of approach to life, if only he had stepped down off his own high-principled horse, he would not have seen these grief-struck strangers as an obstacle to avoid but an opportunity to embrace. If only he had applied the ancient wisdom of the ancient Native Americans.

"Before you judge a man, walk a mile in his moccasins."

Merciful or Mercenary

How easy it is for those of us who call ourselves Christians to be infected with a kind of "summit superiority", to think of ourselves as the kings and queens of the castle, while viewing everyone else as dirty rascals. Having taken the moral high ground, we dismiss and ignore everyone with our judgmental attitude.

> **Like the vicar on the Underground train, we become mercenary rather than merciful, we become soldiers of fortune rather than soldiers of faith.**

How easy it is to demonstrate the attitude of the unmerciful servant that Jesus talked about; having been forgiven much, the man then refused to forgive others (Matthew 18:22-35).

Having been accredited with the righteousness of Christ, we can so easily forget the spiritual darkness and moral depravity from which we have been rescued. At the same time, we can so often forget that righteousness is not just about me being in a right relationship with God; it's about me doing the right thing in my relationship with others and in my outreach to those who have been wronged by life.

When three of Jesus's disciples found themselves on the Mount of Transfiguration, Peter had dogmatic ideas about what should happen next. He wanted to pitch camp and stay on the summit. John would later speak of this luminous and transformational moment. "His clothes shimmered, glistening white, whiter than any bleach could make them. Elijah, along with Moses, came into view, in deep conversation with Jesus" (Mark 9:2-6, MSG). When, for one moment, the divinity of Christ broke through the skin of His humanity, He was joined by the Old Testament heroes, Moses and Elijah. Peter's impetuous response was to bask forever in the glory. "Let's build some booths," he said. "And let's revel in the glory."

History teaches us that Christians tend to set up camp around particular moments of transfiguration. Moments of revelation then become a history of stagnation. Entire denominations start this way.

Trying to contain a moment, they create a movement, but the movement in time becomes a monument, before finally morphing into a museum.

How quickly fiery encounters degenerate into cold traditions!

You could argue that this happened with the Sermon on the Mount. There were many people that day who climbed to the summit of a Galilean hill to be taught the eight angles of approach to kingdom life. Jesus fully intended that these same people should not remain on the mountain talking about these counter-cultural Be-Attitudes but descend with Him into the valleys in order to live them out by continuing to live in a right relationship with the Father and by continuing to right the wrongs of this world. Having found fullness and fulfilment at the summit, how easy it is to want to settle there. We need to recall and apply the words of the accomplished mountaineer, Ed Viesturs, "The summit is just a halfway point."[54] We are on a journey of two halves. It's no good expending all our energy on the ascent, leaving nothing for the descent. While learning to *rely on God* has brought us to the top, all this has been preparatory to our learning how to *relate to others*, (see page 59).

In all this, we must resist the "settler" mentality of Peter; he wanted to set up a tent to contain the glory of God. Peter forgot that God's Presence was not restricted to a tent or temple. In Jesus, the Word had become flesh and moved into the neighbourhood. John, who accompanied Peter, knew this. For him, the Transfiguration was not a call to stagnation. It was a summons to descend into the valleys of the world and proclaim that he and others had beheld the glory of God in Jesus Christ. John's rallying cry was, "We proclaim to you what we have seen and heard, so that you also may have fellowship with us" (1 John 1:3). Rather than making a moment into a monument, John turned it into a mission.

Like the vicar on the train, we can so easily miss the moment because of a totally wrong perspective.

Being merciful is replaced by being mercenary.

Being religious is no substitute for being relational.

---

54. http://climbreport.net/quotes/

From Judgment to Mercy

It is both Pharisaic and hypocritical to imbibe a self-righteous attitude that says, "God, I thank you that I am not like the dad on the train" (Luke 18:11). By its very nature, righteousness is relational. Although it starts with getting right with God, righteousness also means doing the right thing, at the right time, in the right way and righting the wrongs of this world. It means leaning forward and listening, learning to empathize rather than judge. It means committing yourself to showing the Father's love and compassion when a person is in need.

Jesus has some harsh things to say in Matthew 25:14-30 concerning those who, having received from God, sit back idly awaiting the king's return without attending to the needs of the world.

Those who are truly righteous feed the hungry, give drink to the thirsty, open their doors to the stranger, clothe and care for the needy.

Someone has said it well: "An individual has not started living until he can rise above the narrow confines of his individualistic concerns to the broader concerns of all humanity. Every man must decide whether he will walk in the light of creative altruism [regard for others as a principle of action] or the darkness of destructive selfishness. This is the judgment. Life's most persistent and urgent question is, 'What are you doing for others?'"[55]

Christianity must break out of its building-centred mentality. This is a wrong angle of approach to life. Those of us who call ourselves Christians must feel the bleak social winter in

---

55. Coretta Scott King, *The Words of Martin Luther King, Jr.* (HarperCollins, 2001).

which people like the man on the train are suffering in silence a tragedy they have no resources to handle. Christianity must take on flesh and blood, pitch camp in the valleys, and address the relevant issues of the day. The Church cannot remain silent about, or aloof from, issues such as poverty, violence, war, racism, inner-city crime, drugs, disease, child abuse and homelessness. We cannot turn a blind eye to life's harsh realities. We serve a loving, heavenly Father who is "rich in mercy" (Ephesians 2:4). Through new birth, we become partakers "in the divine nature" (2 Peter 1:4). As the sons and daughters of God, we have experienced His mercy, but this is not the end of our journey. Now we are equipped to "show mercy", which is why Jesus says, "Be merciful, just as your Father is merciful" (Luke 6:36). Mercy not only revels in the resources that the Father gives but focuses on the need in the one who needs what we have. Mercy is therefore inseparable from action.

Sympathy

Showing mercy is not just an emotional spasm of pity. Rather, it is a Christ-like attitude by which we deliberately identify ourselves with a person's situation. It is sympathy in the real sense of the word. Sympathy is derived from two words, one that means "together with" and the other "to experience or to suffer". Sympathy therefore means "to be affected by the suffering of another".

The apostle Paul tells us we can approach the throne of grace with confidence because we have in Jesus a Great High Priest in the heavenly realms and this High Priest is not aloof from our pain because He is "touched with the feeling of our infirmities" (Hebrews 4:15, KJV). This heavenly Jesus sympathizes with us, so much so that we can be assured of receiving "mercy . . . to help us in our time of need" (Hebrews 4:16, KJV).

True sympathy is the ability to walk in another man's shoes.

Paul said, "If one part [of the body] suffers, every part suffers with it; if one part is honoured, every part rejoices with it" (1 Corinthians 12:26). Sympathy is a deliberate identification with someone, a desire and determination to see things from their perspective. It is a state in which we "rejoice with those who rejoice, and weep with those who weep" (Romans 12:15, NASB).

To prevent sympathy becoming sentimentality, we should recognize that this angle of approach to life does not mean the following:

- Joining in someone's "pity party".

- Letting unrepentant people off the hook when they have violated God's Word. Mercy does mean overlooking sin. Mercy and truth are often linked together in Scripture.

- Easing the pain but ignoring its cause.

- Being kind in the wrong way and at the wrong time. When Jesus visited the home of Martha and Mary, Mary understood that Jesus wanted peace. Martha, on the other hand, wanted to bless and impress. Both showed sympathy, but only Mary responded appropriately (Luke 10:38-42). How often do we offer kindness in our way and on our terms, whether the other party likes it or not?

When the widow's son died in Zarephath, in her frustration the mother accused Elijah. He responded with love and understanding, not judgment (1 Kings 17:7-24). Later, when he himself was suffering from nervous exhaustion following the victory on Mount Carmel, Elijah begged to die (1 Kings

19:3-4). Jezebel would have gladly done the job for him, but God sympathized with him and sent an angel to feed him supernaturally. Having shown mercy and allowed Elijah to rest, God later cornered him in a cave and applied truth with his various acts of kindness (1 Kings 19:9-18).

Mercy is more than offering encouraging words to people who feel depressed, more than a matter of giving advice to needy people. It is identifying with someone in need to such a degree that you see and hear what that person sees and hears. Sympathy in this respect is a matter of the will. It is a decision to do whatever is necessary to bring a righteous resolution to a situation of need. It is to see the need and by God's grace do the right thing at the right time in the right way in response to that need.

Showing mercy therefore involves:

- Identifying a person's need for them.

- Specific acts of kindness. The Good Samaritan is an example of someone who showed mercy (Luke 10:30-37). While the representatives of orthodox religion passed by the wounded man, the Samaritan "saw him . . . took pity on him . . . bandaged his wounds, pouring on oil and wine. Then he put the man on his own donkey, brought him to an inn and took care of him." Mercy, according to Dr Martyn Lloyd-Jones, means: "pity, plus action".[56]

- Being quick to forgive an offence.

- Releasing people from what you could sometimes rightfully demand. Philemon owed his life to the apostle Paul, who now asked him to reciprocate mercy by treating his runaway slave as he would Paul (Philemon 17).

- Being honest enough to expose root issues and helping people to work through them.

---

56. Martyn Lloyd-Jones, *Studies in the Sermon on the Mount* (IVP, 1971).

Empathy

While on a 10-month lecture tour of America, Nico and Ellen Smith heard Henri Nouwen talking on incarnational theology. What Nouwen said made a lasting impression on both of them. Nouwen explained his theory: "If you really want to minister to the poor, you have to live as they live. You have to be one of them, to experience the same problems, to live the same life, to share the same distresses. Only then can you truly identify with those you have come to serve."

Hooked by what they had heard, the Smiths determined to look further into this teaching. In their search, they came across a book by John Perkins, an African American pastor brought up in the deep South of the USA. Perkins had been beaten almost to death in police cells during the 1970s for his work in the civil rights movement. Nico went through the book entitled *Justice for All*, marking passages that underlined what Henri Nouwen had taught. They included the following:

"If we are going to be the body of Christ, shouldn't we do as he did? He didn't commute daily from heaven to earth to minister to us. Nor did he set up a mission compound which would make him immune to our problems. No, he became flesh and lived among us."

"God didn't have to become a man to find out what our needs were; but we needed him to become man so that we would know he knew our needs. Because he became one of us, we could be sure he understood."

"An outsider can seldom know the needs of the community well enough to know how best to respond to them. Without relocation, without living among the people, without actually becoming one of the people, it is impossible accurately to identify the needs as the people perceive them. Our best attempts to reach people from outside will patronize them."

"Jesus was equal to God, yet he gave that up and took the form of a servant. He took on the likeness of man. He came and lived among us. He was called Immanuel, 'God with us.' The incarnation is the ultimate relocation."[57]

Perkins went on to conclude: "Not only did God relocate among us by taking the form of a man, but when a fellowship of believers relocates into a community, Christ incarnate invades that community. Christ, as his body, as his church, comes to dwell there." This so challenged Nico and Ellen that they became the first Afrikaners to be given governmental permission to live in a black township.

In a world of "cardboard cities", "ethnic minorities" and "inner city crisis", the Church cannot remain either silent or separate.

If we are to become instrumental in establishing God's kingdom in the earth, we must become people who know how to "show mercy".

For some people that may mean relocation, but for all of us it will undoubtedly involve moving out of our cloistered mentality and taking the gospel to the nations. God, who is "full of compassion and mercy" (James 5:11), desires to work through His body, the Church.

The ultimate expression of walking in another man's moccasins was the incarnation – God sending His Son in the likeness of sinful humanity. "For this reason [Jesus] had to be made like his brothers in every way, in order that he might become a merciful and faithful high priest in service to God"

---

57. Rebecca de Saintonge, *Outside the Gate* (Hodder & Stoughton, 1989).

(Hebrews 2:17). God Himself got right inside human skin. He relocated in this world as a man, to see things as we see them, to feel as we feel. He came to identify with men and women to set people free. He is not like the vicar on the train; He shows mercy by "[moving] into the neighbourhood" (John 1:14, MSG).

Empathy is accordingly more than sympathy. The sympathetic person sees what a wounded person sees and feels compassion for them. The empathetic person sees what a wounded person sees and then lives alongside them, feeling what they feel, then responding in a needs-based and organic way.

Merciful Heroes

From an early age, I loved collecting. While most boys were into postage stamps and sports memorabilia, I was into picture postcards depicting great missionaries. Whenever these heroes were home on furlough, they would often stay in our house. They would tell thrilling and sometimes scary stories of their exciting journeys in some far-flung corner of the earth. To my childlike mind, their lives seemed one big adventure story full of travel, danger and the absence of washing facilities! These heroes were willing to leave the comfort of the United Kingdom and set up home in the most appalling conditions. What made them go where no Western person had been before? What drove them to set up schools, hospitals and mission stations miles from civilization? Was it to establish a piece of the British Commonwealth in darkest Africa? Was it to sow Victorian tradition and religious ethics into a foreign culture? I don't think so.

The truth is, many of these ambassadors of the gospel had heard the call to empathize with another culture, to relocate and befriend people. They had no motive other than to show mercy because they themselves had experienced mercy.

Truly, showing mercy will play havoc with your privacy and mess with your destiny.

This desire to show mercy motivated a young housemaid who, though she was refused support from the missionary society, saved enough money for a one-way train ticket to China. Gladys Aylward became a naturalized Chinese citizen, empathizing with the culture. She ate the strange local food and dressed as the Chinese to show mercy to the people of China. William Booth, Albert Schweitzer, David Brainerd, George Müller and many more are likewise classic examples of what it means to show mercy.

In more modern times, Agnes Gonxha Bojaxhiu, or Mother Teresa as she is better known, was a shining example of what it means to exercise this angle of approach to life. Spurred on by an incident in which she found a dying woman whose feet had been half-eaten by rats and ants, she determined to set up a hospice for the terminally ill. She collected people off the streets, from garbage dumps and from under the bridges of Calcutta. She described the purpose of her venture in this way: "We want to make them feel that they are wanted . . . and that there are people who really love them, who really want them, at least for the few hours they may have to live . . . to know human and divine love." On another occasion she said: "The biggest disease today is not leprosy or tuberculosis, but . . . the feeling of being unwanted, uncared for and deserted by everybody."[58]

Christianity has every right to be proud of its social reformers: William Wilberforce, who worked to abolish slavery; the Seventh Earl of Shaftsbury, who looked after chimney-sweep children; Robert Raikes, the father of Sunday

---

58. Kathleen White, *Heroes of the Cross* (Marshall Pickering, 1985).

schools; William Booth and his service to the poor, which started in the East End of London. Yet questions need asking.

What has happened to the social conscience of the Church today?

Are we in danger of becoming so marginalized that we become unmoved by the poverty and injustice around us? Am I willing to hurt with those who are hurting? Have I become so self-sufficient that social issues have no part to play in my comfortable Christianity?

Where are those sons of the kingdom who will empathize with the poor and speak out against the issues of injustice and the ill-treatment of minority groups? Is the Church showing a distinct lack of concern for those less fortunate? Has the Church become a middle-class ghetto, immunized against the effects of the real world? Have we become cocooned in our warm, air-conditioned environment?

May the Lord help us to present a gospel that is relevant and to empathize with the poor and oppressed.

Freedom Workers

"Blessed are the merciful, for they will be shown mercy." Notice the promise. The book of James insists that to be forgiven we must be willing to forgive, for "judgment without mercy will be shown to anyone who has not been merciful" (James 2:13). Perhaps the vicar on the train would have done well to remember that "mercy triumphs over judgement".

The Lord's Prayer continues this same theme when Jesus teaches us to say: "Forgive us our debts, as we also have forgiven our debtors." Jesus adds, "If you forgive men when they sin against you, your heavenly Father will also forgive you. But if you do not forgive men their sins, your Father will not forgive your sins" (Matthew 6:12; 14-15).

If you have ever played the world-famous board game Monopoly, the phrase "Get out of jail free" will be familiar. At various points during the game, you pick up a card with those words on it. If for some reason you happen to be sent to jail, the card allows you immediate release without missing a turn.

Like the Monopoly card, the Be-Attitude of showing mercy is a key to spiritual freedom.

Used correctly, it keeps us free. If it is missing or used wrongly, we risk spiritual, emotional and mental lock-up.

In the parable of the unmerciful servant found in Matthew 18:21-35, we can see the implications of an unmerciful attitude. A wrong attitude is a matter of life and death. Because of this man's unmerciful attitude, his unforgiving spirit, he was "handed . . . over to the torturers until he should repay". Once he had experienced mercy, he should have reciprocated with mercy. Instead, he refused to forgive the one who had offended him. This was contrary to the principles of Matthew 5:23-24. He therefore brought into play another law, the law of checks and balances. "With the measure you use, it will be measured to you" (Matthew 7:2).

Thayer translates the Greek word "torturers" (Matthew 18:34) as drawing out truth "by means of the rack". The idea conveyed is that of a medieval torture in which the individual was strapped to a bench and, with a rope attached to his arms and legs, was stretched until he confessed to the crime he had been accused of committing.

Wouldn't you rather show mercy than receive torture?

Roots and Fruits

A seed of offence sown into the ground of insecurity will soon take root. When we become offended by something a person has said or not said, done or not done, we allow the situation to fester and become blown out of all proportion.

If allowed to settle, a seed of offence will create a root of bitterness which in turn will produce the fruit of resentment (Hebrews 12:15). "Resentment means to feel or to show displeasure at an act, person, remark or situation from a sense of injury or insult."[59] Unresolved relationship issues can imprison a person in resentment, causing a whole host of troubles in his or her life. Resentment is symptomatic of a stubborn attitude and can produce fear (Jeremiah 4:14-19), complaining (Job 7:11) and negative talk (Ephesians 4:31).

The children of Israel were delivered from Egypt to preserve the purity of their beginnings. Yet soon they faced the bitter waters of Marah (Exodus 15:22-27). Getting Israel out of Egypt was relatively easy; getting the bitterness of Egypt out of Israel was much more difficult.

The early church, although brought to birth through the miraculous, had to confront the impure attitude of Ananias and Sapphira (Acts 5:1-11). In the same way, the first priesthood faced its Nadab and Abihu, priests who "offered strange fire before the LORD" (Numbers 3:4, NASB). Cain and Abel faced relational problems too.

God will prepare for Himself a pure church, "a radiant church, without stain or wrinkle or any blemish, but holy and blameless" (Ephesians 5:27). It will be a redeemed community of people who, having experienced mercy, will show mercy to a dying world. Their prayer will be:

---

59. Bob Mumford, *The Prison of Resentment* (Life Changers, 2015).

Lord, make me a channel of thy peace,
that where there is hatred, I may bring love;
that where there is wrong, I may bring the spirit of forgiveness;
that where there is discord, I may bring harmony;
that where there is error, I may bring truth;
that where there is doubt, I may bring faith;
that where there is despair, I may bring hope;
that where there is shadow, I may bring light;
that where there is sadness, I may bring joy.[60]

---

60. A prayer reportedly written by St Francis of Assisi.

GROUP DISCUSSION AND PERSONAL APPLICATION GUIDE

Group Discussion:

- What do you think we could learn from the vicar on the train?

- What is your *neighbourhood* and how do we stay connected with it?

- What are your thoughts about the growth from the seed of offence, via the root of bitterness to the fruit of resentment?

- Do you find the phrase *Jesus moved into the neighbourhood* challenging?

Personal Application:

- Do either of the men on the train resonate with you in any way?

- What might *moving into the neighbourhood* look like for you?

- Have I become so cloistered in my cosy church environment that I am more interest in preserving the past than changing the course of the future?

When it comes to Personal Application we would encourage you to involve a "Spiritual Summiteer" (see page 37) so as to give yourself some level of accountability and guide you on your ongoing journey.

BE-ATTITUDE 6

"Blessed are the pure in heart, for they will see God."

An angle of approach to life that maintains a pure unadulterated drive to show mercy and make peace.

10

MOTIVES MATTER

*"It is very seldom . . . that we do even our finest
actions form absolutely unmixed motives."*
William Barclay[61]

The America's Cup is to yacht-racing what the Ashes are to
cricket and the Superbowl is to American football, so it was a
bitter pill for the American holders when what they considered
as "their cup" was won from them first by Australia in 1983 and
then by New Zealand in 1995. For USA skipper Dennis Conner,
the 1983 defeat was difficult to take. Having gained the privilege
of representing his country, Conner committed the grave
offence of losing the cup for the first time in its 132-year history.

For the next four years, the defeated skipper set about
restoring his country's pride and his own reputation. Conner
coined the phrase "a commitment to the commitment" and
searched for ten men who embraced this same motto from the
hundreds available to him. "I made it clear," he said. "No one
would make the team unless he put winning the cup ahead of
everything else in his life. You have to start with a goal, and
then put everything else aside until you achieve it." Seven
days a week, up to eighteen hours a day, he prepared himself,
his crew and his boat for the ultimate challenge. When asked
about the essential characteristics needed to regain the trophy,
Conner replied, "The three major factors in a successful
crewman are attitude, attitude, attitude."[62]

---

61. William Barclay, *The Daily Study Bible Series* (St Andrew Press, 1978).
62. Dennis Conner, *Comeback: My Race for the America's Cup* (Bloomsbury, 1987).

It is no accident that some people soar above the challenges of life, while others live continually under the pressure of circumstances.

The answer has to do with our motives. Where better to bring up this topic than right in the centre of the teaching on relating to others? "Blessed are the pure in heart" is a kind of divine scan that checks the driving force in our lives, a truth detector that answers a core question: "What is the motive behind your showing mercy and making peace?"

What Drives You to Do What You Do?

Motives are important because motives propel us to action. The word "motive" is derived from the same word as "motor". Just as a motor drives a vehicle, so motives are the propelling force behind the way we act and the direction we take. They motivate us either to act or not. So, the question is, what drives us to do what we do?

The "pure heart" belongs to the person who acts from undiluted, godly motives.

If, for instance, there is any measure of selfishness in our actions, our motives are classed as mixed. What is done for others in the name of Jesus can be tainted by a desire to be seen by others as virtuous (as in "virtue signalling"). In cases like these, our motive is to gain remuneration or win people's applause. Although the action appears good, the motive is mixed and impure, thus undermining its integrity.

A motive is usually described as having a purpose attached, such as "to make money", "to do God's will" or "to be praised by people". No matter what the motivation, it will always produce either overt or covert behaviour. For instance, I may have a deep-seated motivation to become prominent among a certain group of people. I might therefore avoid mixing with those I consider unimportant. I might change my habits and lifestyle to create an acceptable image. My opinions might be altered to agree with those I want to impress. I might build relationships with the in-crowd, hatch schemes and plot how I could open doors otherwise closed to me. Yet, all the time I might be unaware of what I am doing. Such overt behaviour patterns are driven by impure motives. Hence the importance of being pure of heart. "You're blessed when you get your inside world – your mind and heart – put right. Then you can see God in the outside world" (Matthew 5:8, MSG).

"It is very seldom indeed that we do even our finest actions from absolutely unmixed motives."[63]

Let's take evangelism as an example. What is the driving force behind my evangelistic efforts in relation to non-Christians? Am I befriending that neighbour as a means to an end? Do I see him as a project – as potential pew fodder? Have I taken on board the spirit of the age that sees people as "contacts", "numbers", "statistics", "stepping-stones" or "faceless souls"? Do I want to win people to Christ to glorify God, or so that the story of my involvement in their conversion casts me in a good light?

People can so easily become numbers. It is often the case today that people are no longer seen as unique individuals with personal thoughts, feelings, ambitions and needs. While the world may accept such a dehumanizing tendency, the

---

63. William Barclay, *The Daily Study Bible Series* (St Andrew Press, 1978).

Church must guard its heart and have a zero tolerance for such depersonalizing attitudes and motives.

Look at Jesus's motives. Jesus treated the woman at the well with respect even though her life was a mess. He saw her as someone who had personal thoughts, feelings, goals and unrealized ambitions – a unique individual whom God loved (John 4:4-42).

Jesus spoke of those who loved to be announced loudly and who performed their religious deeds in front of the crowd to earn acclamation and approval. He concluded simply: "They have received their reward in full" (Matthew 6:5).

What is the driving force behind your willingness to serve others? If it is to receive public recognition, you had better enjoy the accolades now, for there is no heavenly appreciation society that is going to applaud you in eternity.

True servanthood flows from a pure source, a heart whose motives are clean and clear.

Jesus said: "I am among you as one who serves" (Luke 22:27). Every act of mercy and peace was born out of a pure motivation. His actions were perfect, never for effect. Likewise, Paul wrote to the Ephesians on the issue of serving: "Servants . . . be obedient to those who are your physical masters, having respect for them and eager concern to please them, in singleness of motive and with all your heart, as [service] to Christ [Himself] – not in the way of eye-service [as if they were watching you] and only to please men, but as servants . . . of Christ, doing the will of God heartily and with your whole soul; rendering service readily with goodwill, as to the Lord and not to men" (Ephesians 6:5-7, AMP).

Speaking about mixed motives, Jesus highlights the hypocrites who gave money and prayed so as "to be honoured by men"

(Matthew 6:1-2). It was this kind of serving for effect that Jesus condemned. His comments were directed to people wanting to receive the temporal adoration and appreciation of people, rather than an eternal reward of hearing, "Well done, thou good and faithful servant . . . have thou authority over . . . cities" (Luke 19:11-27, KJV).

The Bible is therefore clear on the matter of motivation. God does not recognize or reward any service that is for

- Self-display
- Prestige
- Respectability
- Superiority
- Self-righteousness
- Building up credits.

Motives such as these are hay and stubble – material that will not stand the fiery test of divine scrutiny.

We can all display magnificent acts of mercy. We may pride ourselves on the walls of hostility that we have dismantled as we have negotiated peace and ministered reconciliation. But if our motives are wrong, we automatically undermine and negate the action. God sees through us: "The LORD does not look at the things man looks at. Man looks at the outward appearance, but the LORD looks at the heart" (1 Samuel 16:7). Only a pure motive will procure the Father's eternal approval.

The finest spiritual act done for self-interest or public applause is judged hypocritical and therefore unfit for purpose.

Jesus teaches His disciples to check the reason why they are doing what they are doing; right motives come from a pure heart.

Motives can, of course, be selfish. Our finest actions can be tarnished by this "me, my and mine" attitude. If what we say and do issues from an independent, self-centred attitude – one that characterizes so much of present, consumerist culture – it becomes unacceptable as service pleasing to the Master.

Motives can also be born from a desire to compromise with the world. What at face value appears to be an act of kindness to an unregenerate person, or a means to promote God's kingdom in society, is actually driven by a friendship with the world which, according to James, is hatred towards God (James 4:4-10).

True motives must be spiritual. Notice, I didn't say "religious". What I am talking about here are actions that arise from the interaction between the Holy Spirit and my spirit. When motives are inspired by the Holy Spirit, we can show God's mercy and bring true peace without there being any selfish, hidden agenda.

Pure Motives

Jesus teaches, "Blessed are the pure in heart." What does the word "pure" mean in this context? The Greek word is *katharos* which could be translated "clean" – as in "the state or condition of having been cleaned". It points to something "free from mixture or anything that soils, adulterates or corrupts". In the ancient world, we find this word being used in different contexts but with the same overtones. When something is *katharos*, it is like unalloyed gold, unmixed wine, or unadulterated milk. The word therefore had a wide application. *Katharos* was even used of an army purged of cowards, dissidents and inefficient soldiers, to produce a first-class fighting force.

Imagine a church like that!

During the days of the communist clamp-down in the Soviet Union, Christians had to meet in secret for fear of imprisonment. One such group, singing and worshipping God in a cabin far away from any town or city, was suddenly interrupted by a heavy banging on the door. All at once, it burst open to reveal a Russian soldier. Fearful for their lives, the people waited to see what would happen next.

"Anyone not willing to give his life for Jesus Christ go outside," he shouted.

A few people left the room. When they had gone, the soldier stepped inside and sat down with the remaining Christians. To their amazement, he said, "I'm a born-again believer. I only want to share fellowship with people who are true Christians, and who are willing to lay down their lives for the kingdom!"

That's what pure in heart means.

It refers to a single-minded, undistracted, uncompromising motivation, expressed through a whole-hearted commitment. In the case of the Russian church, once the soldier entered, the community became *katharos*. It was an army purged of cowards.

In the light of this, we will not be surprised to learn that *katharos* also came to be used in the sense of being "free from what is false or insincere". It described corn that had to be processed in order to separate the chaff from the pure wheat. J.B. Phillips therefore translated this beatitude to reflect this meaning: "Happy are the utterly sincere, for they will see God!" William Barclay rendered it, "Blessed is the man whose motives are always entirely unmixed, for that man shall see God."[64]

By using the word *katharos* (or its Aramaic equivalent), Jesus penetrated the very depths of our being. He shone the searchlight of His love right into the cavernous recesses of the human heart, knowing full well that this is the wellspring for every act of kindness and mercy, every gesture of

---

64. William Barclay, *The Daily Study Bible Series* (St Andrew Press, 1978).

reconciliation and peace. We must therefore guard our hearts. As the Bible says, "Keep thy heart with all diligence; for out of it are the issues of life" (Proverbs 4:23, KJV).

The heart is the centre or seat of a person's moral decisions, the fulcrum of all feelings, the core of one's character.

The Hebrew word translated "heart" literally means "centre". It is the origin of our words and actions, the source from which everything else flows.

It is crucial therefore that we protect the well from which our actions flow. This will avoid mixed motives muddying the waters. We could accordingly paraphrase this Be-Attitude as follows: "Blessed is the man whose heart [his core and centre] is free from all impurities and anything that corrupts."

Creaseless Motives

There is another way of explaining the phrase "purity of heart". As we have seen, it means first and foremost to be clean, free from impurities. But another way of translating it is to say that it is "an undivided heart", or, more literally, "a heart *without folds*".

When the Bible speaks of being pure it refers to sincerity, being transparent and crystal clear. It is the complete opposite to being hypocritical. The hypocrite is like an actor wearing a mask, pretending to be what he or she is not. It is like the person we refer to as "two faced". What is seen is not the true person, but a pretence, an act, a show.

Purity of heart in many ways corresponds with the term "singleness of eye" which Jesus uses later (Matthew 6:19-25, KJV). Again, this means "without folds"; it is open, with nothing hidden. Purity of heart is single-minded or single-eyed devotion.

One of the best definitions of purity is given in Psalm 86:11: "Give me an undivided heart, that I may fear your name." The pure heart is the heart that is no longer divided.

The trouble is that many of us have divided hearts. One part wants to worship God and to please Him, the other wants something else.

That was the psalmist's dilemma concerning his heart. "Make it one", he seems to say. "Make it single, take out the pleats and the folds, let it be whole, let it be one, let it be sincere, let it be entirely free from any hypocrisy."[65]

To be truly pure in heart is to have a singleness of purpose, a resolve to serve one Master, not to act from a hypocritical attitude. If, as Dr Barclay reckoned, many of our finest actions are from impure motives, we need to go back to the ironing board to allow the Holy Spirit to straighten us out; we need to allow Him to remove the creases from the very fabric of our heart so that it is clean.

---

65. Martyn Lloyd-Jones, *Studies in the Sermon on the Mount*, (IVP, 1971).

I may take a piece of folded paper, hold it up and say: "Look how clean this is." But although it is not blemished by any visible marks, it is folded in two. At first you only see a half. When it is opened, you see it in its entirety. There is a crease in the centre of the page. It may be clean, but it is not clear.

Our finest actions may appear at first to be spotless, but a close inspection of the underlying motives reveals that they are mixed.

Purity of heart means that even under the microscopic inspection of God's all-seeing eye our actions are rooted in a motivation that is single-minded not two-faced. For some of us, that kind of scrutiny might mean going back to God to get the creases ironed out of our attitudes and intentions. Maybe that majestic deed done in the name of the Lord had an ulterior motive. Or that act of kindness seemingly done with a noble intention had some repayment clause in the small print.

How often are our good deeds done with mixed motives, a sense of reservation, bias or prejudice? Paul wrote to the Colossians (3:22, KJV), "Servants, obey in all things your masters according to the flesh; not with eyeservice, as menpleasers; but in singleness [sincerity] of heart, fearing God." According to Robert Young, the Greek word "*haplotes*", translated "singleness", literally means "freedom from duplicity".[66]

Singleness or sincerity of heart means "to be open, without ulterior motive, unambiguous (having double meaning), wholehearted, free from pretence". It is the way in which Paul said he had conducted himself in the world and in his

---

66. Robert Young, *Analytical Concordance to the Bible* (Hendrickson, 8th edition, 2007).

relationship with God's people, "with devout and pure motives and godly sincerity" (2 Corinthians 1:12, AMP).

Jesus wants us to embrace the Be-Attitude of integrity.

He declares us blessed if we choose to do everything from a willing and honest intention, not for self-gain or the adulation of others, but with the undiluted and unmixed motive of one who has sold out their heart to think like Jesus.

Why Booster Rockets Fail

Sex scandals, unfaithfulness, perjury, fraud, misappropriation of company funds, welshing on a deal are all symptomatic of a culture that lacks integrity. The ability to keep our promises is fundamental to our survival. It is an issue of life and death.

The horrific explosion of the Challenger space shuttle is permanently engraved on the minds of many Americans. As Christa McAuliffe prepared to be the first civilian on board a NASA space shuttle mission, she had no idea that her life was precariously balanced on the scales of human integrity. That cold January morning, the engineers and designers were locked in an argument about whether the booster seals would work in such low temperatures. The engineers said, "No." Those with greater influence said, "Yes." At 11:39 a.m. on 28th January 1986, just 73 seconds into the flight, Challenger burst into a fireball of smoke, flame and twisted metal.

In his book *Integrity*, Ted Engstrom wrote of this incident: "Power overruled reason. Integrity was the victim. After 70 seconds of flight, a faulty booster rocket ignited millions of gallons of rocket fuel into a blinding explosion. Debris rained on the Florida waters for a solid hour. At first we believed that Christa and the other six crew members perished instantly at the moment of explosion. Upon examination of the cabin remains, we have since learned they may have endured almost three and a half minutes of terrifying freefall before smashing into the Atlantic Ocean at 200 miles per hour. I only wish these words about the urgent need for integrity could carry that same force of impact."[67]

Over the months that followed, a federal investigation unearthed evidence to show that the disaster could have been avoided. NASA had been warned four years earlier that the O-ring booster seals were unreliable. Yet top officials insisted that the programme continue, despite last-minute pleas to postpone the launch. "Before the first shuttle was launched," wrote Ed Magnuson in *Time* magazine, "the agency had known of the fatal seal problem but had buried it under a blizzard of paper while permitting schedule-conscious managers to keep the orbiters flying."[68] Expediency may have won, but integrity was lost.

Integrity means simply doing what we said we would!

The Hebrew word "*tom*" is translated "integrity" in the Old Testament. Its plural form is the word "*thummim*". The same word was used for a part of the High Priest's ceremonial accoutrements used in the Tabernacle of Moses during Israel's wilderness wanderings. "Whenever Aaron enters the Holy Place, he will bear the names of the sons of Israel over his heart on the breastpiece of decision as a continuing memorial before the LORD. Also put the Urim and the Thummim in the breastpiece, so they may be over Aaron's heart whenever he enters the presence of the LORD. Thus Aaron will always bear the means of making decisions for the Israelites over his heart before the LORD" (Exodus 28:29-30).

---

67. Ted Engstrom, *Integrity* (Word, 1988).
68. *Time* magazine, 6th September 1986.

Urim means "lights" and *Thummim* means "perfection". The Urim and the Thummim are steeped in mystery and have been the subject of much debate. While scholars continue to argue over what they were, two things are certain: Aaron was to keep them near to his heart, and they were crucial for making decisions.

This is a picture for Christ followers. We are given the whole armour of God to wear (Ephesians 6:10-20) and one of these pieces is "the breastplate of righteousness" (Ephesians 6:14). In our desire to show mercy and make peace, we need to make sure that our hearts are always right before God, single-minded in devotion, authentic and true. If we do this, our external deeds will issue from a pure heart, an inner source that is both clean and clear of any ulterior or mixed motives.

The Law of Vision

"Blessed are the pure in heart, for they will *see* God." If my action is motivated from a singleness of heart (without mixture, undivided), it will result in an ability to see God's purposes in and through conflicting situations.

While salvation removes the mist of spiritual ignorance, only a purity of heart will facilitate clarity of vision. James throws some light on this attitude when he says, "Purify your hearts, you double-minded" (James 4:8). Where there is mixture, purification has to take place. Remember, "a double-minded man (is) unstable in all he does" (James 1:8). The pure heart is an undivided heart which is why the psalmist's prayer is needed: "Teach me your way, O LORD, and I will walk in your truth; give me an undivided heart, that I may fear your name. I will praise you, O Lord my God, with all my heart" (Psalm 86:11-12). This, as we have already seen, literally means "without folds" – not having mixed motives or double standards, but pure and transparent, with nothing hidden.

We only see what we are able to see. For example, most of us see clusters of lights in the night sky, yet a knowledgeable person calls each star by name, and trans-Atlantic yachtsmen steer their vessels by them. Most of us see clumps of unsightly weeds under the hedgerow, but the botanist sees precious plants that can all be named. Some people see a room full of junk, but the historian sees ancient artefacts.

In a similar way, eight of the Old Testament spies saw giants, the other two saw God. Elisha's servant saw the enemy; Elisha saw the armies of God. Moses saw the one who is invisible (Hebrews 11:27). I'm talking about "the Law of Vision".

If we have a pure heart, we are more likely to see God's purpose in things.

The pure see with God's eyes. Like Joshua and Caleb, they see God driving out the unlawful inhabitants and giving them the land. The others merely see giants and high walls. Joshua and Caleb saw God, not just the natural circumstances. As a result, God fulfilled His promises: "Because my servant Caleb has a different spirit and follows me wholeheartedly, I will bring him into the land he went to, and his descendants will inherit it" (Numbers 14:24). Caleb saw God's plans because he had a wholehearted relationship with God.

Seeing God

An inability to see is restrictive. "Where there is no vision, the people perish", we read in Proverbs 29:18 (KJV). The Hebrew word translated "perish" also means "disintegrate", or "to be unrestrained". The loss of personal vision not only causes chaos and fragmentation, it also destroys our impetus to press forward. If we do not have an ultimate goal in life, we are liable to go off at many different tangents.

Vision helps us to keep going in a prescribed direction and to judge the rights and wrongs of getting involved in various activities. Moses turned his back on a privileged lifestyle and joined himself to his own people "because he saw him who is invisible". Vision is focus; it gives perspective in a situation or circumstance.

Joseph monitored his own life according to a vision he received as a teenager. His success, even in adverse circumstances, was due in no small part to his dream. At the close of his life, he gave strict instructions concerning his mortal remains: the children of Israel were to carry his bones for forty years until they entered the promised land. Why? Because he had caught a vision of God's purposes and it had become his ultimate goal.

Vision is the driving force that keeps us pressing on even in desperate circumstances.

Abraham pursued his destiny in life because he had caught a glimpse of something eternal. "By faith Abraham, when called to go to a place he would later receive as his inheritance, obeyed and went . . . he made his home in the promised land like a stranger in a foreign country; he lived in tents, as did Isaac and Jacob, who were heirs with him of the same promise. For he was looking forward to the city with foundations, whose architect and builder is God" (Hebrews 11:8-10).

In the late 1960s, American Aerospace noted how the principle of vision and motivation worked among its employees. Faced with the challenge of putting a man on the moon, the company saw average employees demonstrating extraordinary levels of performance. Yet once that mission was achieved, performance slumped. Vision causes ordinary people to do extraordinary things.

If the principle is clear and the practice follows, the promise will ensure that "they shall see God!" An undivided heart does not have mixed motives or double standards but is pure and transparent with nothing hidden. Such a heart will see God in all situations.

Corrie Ten Boom beautifully illustrates how being pure of heart leads you to see God in all circumstances. In World War II, Corrie, together with thousands of other prisoners, was transferred to a new death camp at Ravensbrück in Germany. They were housed in harrowing conditions including wooden bunks, straw mattresses and fouled blankets. But that was not all. Once they had managed to climb on to the second level of a three-tier bunk, they found that their beds were infested with fleas!

Corrie seemed unperturbed by the situation. Turning to her sister Betsie, she excitedly related a way in which they could see God in this situation. The fleas would become the means of keeping the prison guards at bay. As a result, both ladies began to give thanks. The circumstances hadn't changed, but from a pure heart they saw God through the overcast and stormy environment of the death camp.

Caleb, as we have already observed, showed "a different attitude" from the rest of the spies (bar Joshua), even when faced by considerable opposition. He and Joshua saw the same opposing factors that the ten other spies saw, but unlike the others they also saw God. The ten saw the giants in the land and said: "We seemed like grasshoppers in our own eyes, and we looked the same to them" (Numbers 13:33). Joshua and Caleb, on the other hand, said: "Do not be afraid of the people of the land, because we will swallow them up. Their protection is gone, but the LORD is with us. Do not be afraid of them"

(Numbers 14:9). Caleb, with a different attitude, could see God during great opposition.

Here, then, we have an angle of approach that will enable us to see God in the darkest of circumstances.

The person with mixed motives sees trouble but misses God; the person who is pure in heart sees God and is not distracted by troubles!

Purity of heart is therefore invaluable for showing mercy and making peace. In actions such as these, we are led to ask whether our motives are mixed or sincere. So often we put on the garments of servanthood, only to realize that our intentions are not altogether pure.

Whenever we ask such soul-searching questions, we go back to the ironing board. Our prayer is this: "Father, help us to be spurred into action by motives that are pure." If our motives are mixed, then we need to allow God to remove the creases and iron-out any insincerity.

GROUP DISCUSSION AND PERSONAL APPLICATION GUIDE

Group Discussion:

- Does Dennis Conner and his view of attitude resonate with any people groups you are involved in?

- Would you agree that mixed motives might harm even our grandest gestures?

- How would you define integrity?

- Would surrounding ourselves with pure-minded people help create a culture of right motives?

Personal Application:

- Are there any creases that need ironing out of your Christian activities?

- When I try to reach those without faith in God, do I tend to treat people as projects?

When it comes to Personal Application we would encourage you to involve a "Spiritual Summiteer" (see page 37) so as to give yourself some level of accountability and guide you on your ongoing journey.

BE-ATTITUDE 7

"Blessed are the peacemakers,
for they will be called sons of God."

A willingness to stand in the gap and
resolve issues from a godly perspective.

11

MIND THE GAP

"Peacemakers are the mercy of God to a sinful world.
They embody His very kindness."
Heidi Baker[69]

Although we might think that self-isolating and social distancing are new phenomena, we would be wrong. Travel back in time to the quaint village of Eyam in Derbyshire, and you will discover that these preventative practices were implemented in the seventeenth century. A plague that had been decimating the city of London made its way to the village. Something had to be done to prevent the disease spreading.

Such was the terror that accompanied this plague that before the lockdown was implemented, those who could fled to family and friends, but Thomas Stanley, a nonconformist minister, and the Reverend Williams Mompesson, decided to stay and serve the people. Taking it upon themselves to lead the way, these two local ministers worked together to quarantine the whole village. As they implemented a programme of self-isolation, doctors tried to stamp out the epidemic. The healthy and the sick were shut up together and their doors marked with a red cross. When venturing out, people were encouraged to wear masks. A stone circle was placed around the village and no one was allowed in or out. Food was left for the villagers at various points and payment was placed in running streams to cleanse the coins. Helped by the harsh winter of 1666 it took fifteen months for the plague to cease. Out of a population of 350 villagers, 260 died.

---

69. Heidi Baker, *Compelled by LOVE* (Charisma House, 2008).

In among the tombstones of Eyam parish church, a simple stone monument was erected in memory of Thomas Stanley. The memorial reads: "He stood between the dead and the living; and the plague was stayed. Numbers chapter 16, verse 48." In a health crisis of pandemic proportions, two leaders laid their lives on the line for others. They employed a Kingdom Be-Attitude to bring an end to a traumatic episode in the lives of their fellow villagers. They exercised the true role of the peacemaker.

Although this idea is only mentioned twice in the whole of the New Testament (Matthew 5:9; James 3:18), there is no reason to believe that the role of the peacemaker is trivial or obsolete. Society is degenerating everywhere. Conflicts are frequently presented on our news media, both national and global. The nuclear family is in freefall. There is religious, ethnic and sectarian division everywhere. The world desperately needs peacemakers today, now more than ever. We need men and women who, like Stanley and Mompesson, will stand in the gap.

> We need divine go-betweens, people who actively involve themselves in the process of bringing God's peace into a divided society.

Troublemakers, Truce-makers and Peacemakers

The New Testament ministry of peace-making does not simply advocate the promotion of human well-being, nor does it merely point others to a place where they might find peace with God. It is far more than that. The task of the peacemaker and peacekeeper requires the active involvement of a third party to step between contentious people to restore God's peace. Peace-making is therefore costly in time, effort and emotional strain. It calls for a self-sacrificial involvement in situations of strife and tension.

The opposite of peace-making is troublemaking. Some people always seem to become "the eye of the hurricane" wherever they go. They either cause an argument or become part of it. They are quarrelsome, touchy, sensitive and defensive – *bona fide* "troublemakers". Speaking of such people, the Bible warns us to be on our guard, to watch, mark, correct and, if necessary, avoid them (Romans 16:17; Titus 3:10; 1 Thessalonians 5:13, 15).

At the other end of the spectrum there are those who hate conflict and will avoid confrontation at all costs. Their motto is "anything for a quiet life" and their approach is one of appeasement, compromise, evading the issue or pacifying. They bite their tongue rather than say what they really think. This person is a "truce-maker".

In Matthew 5:9, Jesus neither condones the troublemaker nor commends the truce-maker. He calls for peacemakers – godly individuals who see their role as bridge-builders, go-betweens, middlemen and mediators for the purpose of making and keeping peace, both inside and outside the Church.

Peacemakers have a creative ability to bring a calming influence on others. This ability is a direct result of the godly manner whereby they conduct their own lives. They are not passive bystanders but aggressive arbiters laying their lives on the line to bring a righteous solution. In seeking to quantify the role of a peacemaker, Bob Mumford has said: "It isn't necessarily a matter of words, though these may be involved at times. It is rather, when you walk into a situation where sparks are flying and tempers are short – does the situation get better or worse?"[70]

---

70. Bob Mumford, *The King and You* (Fleming H. Revell, 1974).

The Peace of God

The basic message of these industrious individuals is "peace". While the peacemaker is the channel, the contents of his/her role is peace. In secular terms, peace is often viewed simply as "the cessation of war or freedom from conflict". This somewhat negative notion of peace is a poor cousin to the Hebrew idea of *shalom*. Peace, or *shalom*, is a godly virtue, deriving from "the God of peace" (Romans 15:33; 16:20; Philippians 4:9). The biblical view of peace is more than the mere absence of conflict. God's peace is never simply a negative state – the absence of trouble. Rather, it is a positive, fully orbed condition containing wealth, health and general well-being. It is peace, but not as the world knows it (John 14:27). It is a "peace that transcends human understanding" (Philippians 4:7, TPT). The Old Testament word translated "peace" (*shalom*) involves the total well-being of an individual. It includes good health and prosperity, leading to a life of tranquillity and contentment. The recipient of this peace is complete – materially, physically, emotionally and spiritually. Let's look at three aspects of this *shalom*: health, wealth and welfare.

1) Health

When he was reunited with his brothers, Joseph demonstrated a godly attitude to those who had so cruelly mistreated him. He asked first after their health (Genesis 43:27). He then asked: "How is your aged Father?" In both instances he used a word or phrase translated from the Hebrew *shalom*. *Shalom* was used as a Jewish greeting. It is usually translated "peace" but it also conveys the idea of harmony, prosperity and fully orbed, positive blessing.

Being at peace within himself, Joseph could extend peace to others.

Enjoying an inner state of health and harmony, he could exude these qualities to his brothers, so that his whole family could enjoy health and harmony. His redemptive attitude to life was consumed with a godly passion and constrained by a Christ-like love, to seek out, raise up and bring back what was lost – healthy and harmonious family relationships.

2) Wealth

In God's economy, peace is a priceless and comprehensive commodity. The psalmist talks about a God "who delights in the prosperity of His servant" (Psalm 35:27, NASB). The word translated "prosperity" is the Old Testament word *shalom*. The prophet Isaiah goes on to endorse this when he declares God's will for His people: "The LORD says: 'I will extend peace to her like a river, and the wealth of nations like a flooding stream'" (Isaiah 66:12). God's peace is intimately associated with the financial well-being of His people.

3) Welfare

Jeremiah suffered much during his prophetic ministry, having been thrown into dungeons and a disused well. The officials of King Zedekiah didn't believe his words were conducive to the people's well-being. "This man is not seeking the good of these people but their ruin," they moaned (Jeremiah 38:4). The word "good" is *shalom* and implies welfare and well-being. There are instances in the Bible where the peace of God conveys the same idea. It is the peacemaker's role and responsibility to involve himself/herself actively in society to mediate, arbitrate, reconcile, negotiate and intercede to bring godly peace where there is no peace. Those who engage in restoring health, wealth and welfare to people in turmoil and conflict are called by Jesus "the sons of God".

Peace-making Personified

The one whose birth brings "peace on earth" was Himself "the Prince of Peace". He had a calming influence on those who followed Him. He brought peace of mind to those who were demonised by the devil. He comforted those who were sick, bereaved and dying. He stilled the storm and calmed the sea. Religious leaders tried to embroil Him in the spiritual arguments of the day, but Jesus revealed His divine capacity for peace-making by reconciling seemingly irreconcilable differences: "Give to Caesar what is Caesar's, and to God what is God's" (Luke 20:25). Supremely, Jesus made peace on the cross for all humankind by Himself bearing the brunt of people's cruelty. Yet "He uttered no threats, but kept entrusting Himself to Him who judges righteously" (1 Peter 2:23, NASB). As the Prince of Peace, Jesus reconciled to "himself all things, whether things on earth or things in heaven, by making peace through his blood, shed on the cross" (Colossians 1:20). He is the peacemaker par excellence, breaking down "the barrier, the dividing wall of hostility" between human beings and God, and between human beings and each other (Ephesians 2:14-22).

Thanks to the cross, there is no separation between Gentiles and Jews. Gentiles are "no longer foreigners and aliens [to the promises and purpose of God], but fellow-citizens with God's people and members of God's household". As citizens of God's kingdom and viceroys of His victory, Gentile and Jewish believers in Jesus make peace by being the vehicle through whom the message of the gospel is spread.

Our aim is to see men and women reconciled to God, making their peace with Him and each other.

When it comes to peace-making, our desire is to arbitrate, to reconcile, to stand as Moses did between the dead and the living and stop the plague of division (Numbers 16:47-48). Our role is to act as an impartial third party, moving between two disputing or conflicting factions, just as Jesus has already done in His work on the cross.

Peacemakers and peacekeepers, to be effective, need to be wise, understanding, "pure . . . peaceable, gentle, reasonable, full of mercy and good fruits, unwavering, without hypocrisy", approachable, full of tolerance and kind actions, with no breath of favouritism or hint of hypocrisy (James 3:17-18, NASB). Again, like so many of the Be-Attitudes introduced by Jesus and amplified by His stepbrother James, a peacemaker is:

- Wise – judges situations without human prejudice

- Pure – intervenes with right motives

- Peaceable – sets a good example

- Gentle – handles people sensitively

- Reasonable – fair

- Full of mercy – able to empathize and extend forgiveness

- Unwavering – sticks with decisions and sees people through difficult times

- Without hypocrisy – practices what he/she preaches

Above all, a peacemaker must be at peace within themselves. They have tasted the peace that results from being filled with the righteousness of Christ. They then desire to produce that same quality of peace in an environment where injustice and unrighteousness rule.

Spheres of Peace-making

In the domain of family life, the parent is often the peacemaker. Here the peacemaker mediates godly peace within the context of family conflicts. As Christ's representative, the peacemaker brings *shalom*, not just for the sake of peace and quiet, but so that the rule of God is extended in the home, so that the family may see His blessing restored.

In the domain of society, the citizen who plays the part of a peacemaker desires to become involved in issues of injustice and unrighteousness, which are often the result of Satan's covert activities in the community. In line with the ethos of Christian peace-making outlined in the Sermon on the Mount, the sons (and daughters) of God are called to create transforming initiatives designed to bring peace in the world.

> We are not merely to protest against an injustice; we are to involve ourselves in grace-filled initiatives that deliver people from being wronged.

Some people would prefer to marginalize Jesus's teachings as an impossible dream with unrealistic demands, totally impractical for today's society. Others see the Sermon on the Mount as the heavenly blueprint for peace-making in the world today. For example, some Christian organizations are experimenting with alternative ways of rehabilitating criminals. They are demonstrating a true ministry of peace-making through reconciliation. Their victim-offender reconciliation programme serves as a go-between. It brings victims and offenders together to pave the way for offenders to make some measure of restitution for the crime and seek reconciliation with the victim.

Through such initiatives, citizens of God's kingdom are being used to bring an end to problems such as social injustice and inner-city deprivation. No wonder creation cries, "Bring on the sons of God!" They alone can establish peace where there is no peace. The ministry of reconciliation – bringing two parties together for the purpose of renewing friendship after a period of estrangement – is an integral part of peace-making. Paul picks up this theme when he writes, "God . . . reconciled us to himself through Christ and gave us the ministry of reconciliation: that God was reconciling the world to himself in Christ, not counting men's sins against them. And he has committed to us the ministry of reconciliation. We are therefore Christ's ambassadors" (2 Corinthians 5:18-20).

Peacemakers seek to reconcile and, as such, they take on the following roles: mediators, intercessors and arbitrators.

1) Mediators

A mediator acts as a go-between for two or more parties. This is something else in which Christ is involved. Paul reminded Timothy, "There is one God and one mediator between God and men, the man Christ Jesus, who gave himself as a ransom for all men" (1 Timothy 2:5-6). The ransom here refers to the price paid to redeem a slave. Christ mediated between God and humanity in giving His life as the ransom price to free us from slavery to sin.

Similarly, the Old Testament priest was to mediate, to bear the needs and requirements of one to the other as appropriate. Jesus alone now has this office as the great high priest who represents us before the throne of God (Hebrews 8:1, 6). Peter reminds the Church that they, too, form a royal priesthood. Just as Jesus is the Great High Priest, the Mediator between earth and heaven, so we are mediators too (1 Peter 2:5). Just as our friends Mike and Jean offer their home as a safe place for married couples facing conflict. Within this non-judgmental environment, each couple finds freedom to share their concerns and experience the wise counsel and prayer ministry from two godly mediators.

We are peacemakers. We act as go-betweens, bringing two estranged parties together.

---

2) Intercessors

Perhaps the most important unseen work of a peacemaker is the ministry of intercession. As an intercessor, the peacemaker pleads the case of another before a higher authority who holds the power to improve that party's position.

During His earthly life, Jesus offered up prayers and petitions (Hebrews 5:7). Today, Jesus forever intercedes before the Father, and the Holy Spirit connects us in our spirits to the prayers of Jesus (Romans 8:26, 34). Those who take on the role of peacemakers as "sons of God" must learn how to intercede with the Holy Spirit. They must learn to plead the case of another before our heavenly Father, for He alone holds the power to bring peace to those caught up in life's conflicts. Paul teaches his son in the faith, Timothy, that a priority for peacemaking is that "first of all . . . requests, prayers, intercession and thanksgiving be made for everyone" (1 Timothy 2:1). This relates to every sphere, including the home.

It must have been hard for my parents to handle me as a rebellious teenager, especially having brought me up in the ways of the Lord. I refused to listen to my parents' advice.

My conflict of interest between the world and God's kingdom became all-consuming. The world began to take more and more spiritual territory, sapping my time, money and energy. But my mother, undeterred, took the matter to God in prayer. She desperately wanted to bring peace to my warring spirit. As a result, intercession became her weapon of warfare. By God's grace and the efforts of a praying mother, I came to heel and committed my life to God once more.

As I thumbed through my mother's King James Bible, given to me after her death, I began to read various marginal notes she had written during her times of prayer. Next to Psalm 138:8 ("The Lord will perfect that which concerneth me"), she had written three simple words: "Concerned for Christopher." Praise God for all the peacemakers who take up the burden of intercession on behalf of others!

3) Arbitrators

The arbitrator is a peacemaker appointed by two parties to settle a dispute between them. Like Kay, a member of our church, who was invited by a troubled teenager into her senior school to arbitrate between the headteacher and her parents. Living under the threat of expulsion the teenager looked on in amazement as Kay brought about a long-term, peaceful resolve acceptable to all concerned.

Job called for an arbiter who would assist him in pleading his innocence and the injustice of his plight (Job 9:32-33). The arbiter's mission is to settle a dispute, to stop a conflict. In biblical terms, cessation of hostilities is the bottom line, while total well-being is the aim.

Based on the principles of Matthew 5:23-24 and 18:15-20, the process of arbitration involves (a) encouraging the conflicting parties to resolve their dispute on their own in private. If that doesn't work, (b) a peacemaker is called for. If necessary, (c) the parties may call on the church to arbitrate, both parties of the dispute agreeing to abide by the church's impartial judgment.

If we ignore this biblical process in resolving interpersonal conflict, we run the risk of spiritual, mental and emotional lockup. Like the unmerciful servant handed over to the torturers, the results of refusing the efforts of peacemakers who seek to bring godly wholeness and well-being can be devastating.

Peacemakers or Peace-lovers?

There is a world of difference between a peace-lover and a peacemaker. Most people are peace-lovers, but because peace-making involves confrontation, conflict and tension, peace-making is less popular because it requires a willingness to make yourself vulnerable. Most people seem unwilling to get involved. They are not ready to experience what it means to be powerless, unprotected and, at times, the focus of vented frustrations. They would much prefer to love peace than make peace.

Peacemakers must allow others to speak their mind. They must be willing to listen and discuss. They must not be threatened when they hear ideas alien to their own. Above all, they must be free from any preconceptions. The aim is not peace at any price. There can be no true reconciliation, no genuine peace, without justice.

The peacemaker is a middleman. He/she listens to both parties in a dispute and encourages them to meet and discuss what is righteous and just. Biblically speaking, there is a strong link between peace and righteousness. The former is dependent on the presence of the latter. Isaiah says: "The fruit of righteousness will be peace; the effect of righteousness will be quietness and confidence for ever" (Isaiah 32:17). From righteousness – the state and standing of being right before God – comes peace. Therefore, a life lived in a way that is acceptable to God will produce the fruit of peace. This will be evident initially by an inner quietness and strength, for "those who walk uprightly enter into peace" (Isaiah 57:2).

The psalmist further emphasizes this bond when using that beautiful phrase "righteousness and peace kiss each other" (Psalm 85:10). This marital symbolism indicates the covenantal relationship between the two. Not only will a godly person live at peace with God, they will reproduce after their own kind.

The natural product of a life in harmony with God is a progeny of peace – offspring that will be peacemakers.

It is not surprising, then, that Paul entreats Timothy to pursue "righteousness, faith, love and peace . . . out of a pure heart" (2 Timothy 2:22). Righteousness becomes a prerequisite for acquiring and maintaining peace in a person's life. Apart from squaring the relationship with God at the outset, righteousness itself calls for a complete change in behaviour to bring it into line with the Word of God. Peace cannot be divorced from a righteous lifestyle; outside of God, peace cannot exist.

From a biblical perspective, conflicts within society demonstrate the absence of righteousness. If this precondition isn't met, the fruit isn't produced. Our prayer is: "God, raise up anointed peacemakers who, with godly wisdom, will bring an answer to the family, the Church and the nation!" Here's the job description!

WANTED: Peacemakers! Urgently needed – people who are clean-living, peace-loving, courteous, considerate, open to reason, full of compassion, wholehearted, straightforward, impartial, free from doubts and insincerity. WANTED: Peacemakers who sow in peace and reap a harvest of righteousness. Immediate start. Training provided. Excellent prospects. Apply within.

The peacemaker is motivated by an inner desire to see God's peace made and maintained in every sphere of human life.

"Make every effort to keep the unity of the Spirit through the bond of peace," writes the apostle Paul (Ephesians 4:3). We are to eagerly strive for and earnestly guard the binding power of peace, for it is peace that undergirds the work of God and society at large. Like the ligaments that bind together the various parts of the human body (Ephesians 4:16), so the peace of God will avert a dislocation in the family, Church and nation ("ligament" is the same word as "bond"). Just as mortar acts as a bonding agent for a brick building, and as a cable holds a ship secure to its moorings, so peace holds together the very fabric of civilization.

It is a fundamental role and responsibility of every child of the King to make and maintain God's peace. Jesus told us to embrace the Be-Attitude of peace-making because He knew that this is a redemptive way of thinking that seeks to restore what was lost. It is an angle of approach to everyday life that buys up opportunities to bring harmony, prosperity and fully orbed blessing to those in conflict.

Like Father, Like Son!

When Scripture refers to someone as a "son" of something or someone, it often means that the two have the same character or nature. So, the term "son of God" designates and marks out a Godlikeness in the person described. Judas is called "son of perdition" (John 17:12, KJV); Barnabas "son of encouragement" (Acts 4:36); James and John "sons of thunder" (Mark 3:17). In each case, "son of" indicates that the person partakes of the quality designated and demonstrates that same vice or virtue in their relationship with others.

In all these cases, the people concerned live up to their names by the way they behave. This is especially true of those who are called "sons of God". Those who demonstrate the Be-Attitude of peace-making are called sons of God because they act like their heavenly Father, who establishes peace and seeks to be at peace with all men and women.

Although the ministry of the "peacemaker" is mentioned only twice in the New Testament, this should not imply that it is a minor role or an insignificant task.

Jesus Himself recognized the fact that peace, when sown, would reap a harvest of righteousness or right standing before God. We bear the title "sons of God". This equates our ministry with that of Jesus Himself. He embodied the role of a peacemaker and united two irreconcilable world groups – the Jews and the Gentiles: "His purpose was to create in himself one new man out of the two, thus making peace, and in this one body to reconcile both of them to God through the cross, by which he put to death their hostility. He came and preached peace to you who were far away and peace to those who were near" (Ephesians 2:15-17). By breaking down the dividing wall that separated Jew and Gentile, Jesus made a way by which non-Jewish men and women could become parties to the covenant of promise.

No wonder, then, that the angels declared at the birth of Christ: "Glory to God in the highest, and on earth peace among men with whom He is pleased" (Luke 2:14, NASB). Jesus alone brings peace to the world. But He has given His ministry of reconciliation and peace-making to us! The angel's declaration can therefore only be fully realized as God's redeemed community take up the challenge of becoming peacemakers.

In war-torn, degenerating societies, the Church has been given a mandate to make and maintain peace.

"Let us therefore make every effort to do what leads to peace and to mutual edification" (Romans 14:19). The world scene is set. Bring on the sons of God, for they alone are charged with the call to bring much needed *shalom*. One of the hallmarks of the sons of God is peace-making. That they partake of this ministry is a sure sign of their sonship. Are you willing to stand in the epicentre of conflict and, from a standpoint of justice and righteousness, arbitrate, mediate, negotiate and intercede in order to reconcile two opposing factions?

According to Scripture, Jesus will return not to a weak minority but to a strong, vibrant, influential body of committed Christians. The Church will comprise believers who are exercising an impact on the world. The Father will recognize His sons and daughters by the degree to which they are making and maintaining His *shalom*.

If an answer is to be found for the conflicts facing today's world, Christian peacemakers – who are themselves living in the Father's *shalom* – must arise. Creation groans, waiting for the immediate as well as the ultimate revelation of "the sons of God" (Romans 8:19). Why? Because the sons of God are peacemakers and, as such, they possess the antidote for a globe in crisis and in conflict.

A Final Checklist

Peacemakers are willing to:

- Confront issues of injustice and unrighteousness
- Become involved in the grime and grit of conflict
- Empathize with both parties in an argument
- Become vulnerable
- Allow others to speak their mind and not be threatened by ideas alien to their own
- Listen and maintain a right attitude
- See issues from God's perspective

Peace-making also involves:

- Being at peace with yourself and God
- Righteous indignation
- Reconciliation
- Negotiation
- Mediation
- Intercession

GROUP DISCUSSION AND PERSONAL APPLICATION GUIDE

Group Discussion:

- Who is your go-to example when thinking about a peacemaker?

- Where is the conflict that you are presently being called on to bring peace?

- How important is trust when involving ourselves in conflict resolution?

- What do you find most challenging from the above checklist for peacemakers?

Personal Application:

- Faced with a plague, would your first thought be to run, or to remain and do whatever is necessary?

- In the eye of a relational storm, would people think of you as a truce-maker or a peacemaker?

When it comes to Personal Application we would encourage you to involve a "Spiritual Summiteer" (see page 37) so as to give yourself some level of accountability and guide you on your ongoing journey.

BE-ATTITUDE 8

"Blessed are those who are persecuted because of righteousness, for theirs is the kingdom of heaven."

A constructive approach to persecution that sees it as the world's way of making a positive ID of who we are.

12

THERE MAY BE TROUBLE AHEAD

"The difference between an obstacle and an opportunity
[is] our attitude toward it. Every opportunity has a
difficulty and every difficulty has an opportunity."
J. Sidlow Baxter[71]

With a spring in their step, the two clergymen made their way through the crowded streets of 16th-century Oxford. The two men in question were Hugh Latimer, the Bishop of Worcester, and Nicholas Ridley, the Bishop of London. The year was 1555. The first man was escorted by the mayor and town alderman, while the second – a close friend and colleague of the first – followed behind. Turning to his companion behind, the first man enquired if he was heading in the same direction.

"As fast as I can," he replied.

To the casual observer, the cheery words and general behaviour of these two Christians would have meant little, except when the onlooker realized that they were both knowingly heading towards an appointment with death. These eminent theologians of their day had been arrested and sentenced to death for their Christian beliefs. Although they were innocent of the charges, they purposefully picked their way through the crowds that lined the pavements to meet their executioner.

Death waited and, "for the joy that was set before them", they hastened to embrace it. Theirs was not to be the relatively quick death of a bullet, a hangman's noose or an electric chair.

---

71. J. Sidlow Baxter, *Awake, My Heart* (Zondervan, 1960).

What awaited them was a medieval form of capital punishment in which the victim was publicly stripped and chained to a wooden stake that had been securely fixed in the ground. He or she would then be surrounded by bundles of firewood and forced to suffer the excruciating torture of being burned alive.

As they arrived at the place of execution, Ridley walked over to where Latimer stood, embraced him and said, "Be of good heart, for God will strengthen us."

After they refused to take a final opportunity to denounce their Christian beliefs, the order was given to chain both men to a stake and for the funeral pyre to be lit. The wood was piled around each of them, with their persecutors standing by to watch.

As the executioner was about to place the torch at Ridley's feet, Latimer turned to his friend and said, "Be of good comfort, Mr Ridley, and play the man. We shall this day light such a candle, by God's grace, in England as I trust shall never be put out."

As the founding fathers of the Anglican Church, the lasting impact of these two historic figures cannot not be understated.

We Will Have Trouble

Eugene Peterson paraphrased Jesus's final Be-Attitude thus:

"You're blessed when your commitment to God provokes persecution. The persecution drives you even deeper into God's kingdom. Not only that – count yourselves blessed every time people put you down or throw you out or speak lies about you to discredit me. What it means is that the truth is too close for comfort and they are uncomfortable. You can be glad when that happens – give a cheer, even! – for though they don't like it, *I* do! And all heaven applauds. And know that you are in good company. My prophets and witnesses have always gotten into this kind of trouble." (Matthew 5:10-12, MSG)

The longer I live, the more I believe conflict is inevitable for Christians.

In immense opposition, Paul and Barnabas sought to strengthen the disciples in Lystra, Iconium and Antioch, "encouraging them to remain true to the faith," saying, "We must go through many hardships to enter the kingdom of God" (Acts 14:22). Paul's personal catalogue of hardships included imprisonment, severe flogging, exposure to death, five times receiving 39 lashes, being beaten with a rod, being stoned, shipwrecked, in danger from false brothers and bandits, hunger, thirst, cold and nakedness (2 Corinthians 11:23-27).

Paul informs the Philippian church that "it has been granted to you on behalf of Christ not only to believe on him, but also to suffer for him" (Philippians 1:29). He then goes on to parallel their angle of approach to suffering with that of Jesus: "Have this attitude in yourselves which was also in Christ Jesus" (Philippians 2:5, NASB).

Although some Christians view opposition as negative, the Bible teaches that conflict can be positive.

In fact, it would be fair to say that some difficulties are not only natural but, in the long term, beneficial. Paul had a positive attitude to persecution: "I delight in weaknesses, in insults, in hardships, in persecutions, in difficulties. For when I am weak, then I am strong" (2 Corinthians 12:10). Opposition, far from being a stranger to Paul, was an expected reaction to righteousness. James, an advocate of the same angle of approach to life, writes: "When all kinds of trials and temptations crowd into your lives my brothers, don't resent them as intruders, but welcome them as friends! Realise that they come to test your faith and to produce in you the quality of endurance" (James 1:2-3, JBP).

World Without Conflict

In his book *The Time Machine*, H.G. Wells described an imaginary future very different from our own. It is an environment free from weeds and fungi, where nettles don't sting, and the summer evening air is free from mosquitoes. In this seemingly idyllic environment, the entire population lives in splendid homes and everyone wears expensive clothes. There is no sign of either social or economic struggle and the necessity for work has been eliminated. Disease has been stamped out and people live in perfect security in an earth where violence is rare. Yet, in what some might call paradise, Wells observed that the removal of hardship, discomfort, violence, wild beasts and the threat of conflict had produced a weak, insipid, spineless generation. The weak remained weak and the strong had no need of their strength. The result was a society that was physically, intellectually and emotionally debilitated. In such an environment people became idle, easily fatigued, lacking in interest and quickly discouraged. Commenting on this science-fictional scenario, Wells said: "We are kept keen on the grindstone of pain and necessity."

Martin Luther King had his dream, but I have a recurring nightmare. In it I see babies born in Christian hospitals and Christian parents sending children to Christian schools, to learn from Christian teachers and to play with other Christian children. This apparent spiritual utopia promotes Christian businesses for Christian workers and encourages Christian holidays in Christian theme parks.

This is not what Jesus had in mind!

I'm not saying that Christian institutions in themselves are wrong. But if such a lifestyle is the embodiment of a ghetto mentality that views the world as a no-go area, then the Church is in trouble. If furnishing the household of faith with such luxury items further comforts and consoles an already cocooned Christianity, then "judgment [must] begin with the family of God" (1 Peter 4:17).

In the same way, if, in the local church, we maintain a homegroup structure that plays host to a weekly pity party, this is a dysfunctional system that panders to the immature cries of an "I want" generation. If we persistently redecorate our manmade structures to cater for inhouse needs, we are papering over the cracks of our foundational flaws.

If we pander to the whims and fancies of a smug, self-satisfied people, we are merely rearranging the deckchairs on an ill-fated _Titanic_.

For some people, the word "church" has become synonymous with comfort. It denotes a haven from a nasty world, a place characterized by "cocooning" – a behaviour defined as "the impulse to go inside when it just gets too tough and scary outside".[72] However, the apostle Paul reminds us that "everyone who wants to live a godly life in Christ Jesus will be persecuted" (2 Timothy 3:12). Persecution for the righteous is natural; it is part of life's process of development. As the botanist watches the emerging caterpillar struggle from its chrysalis, he or she may be tempted to quicken the process by cutting the creature free. But during those moments of struggle, a secretion is

---

72. Faith Popcorn, _The Popcorn Report_ (HarperReference; Reprint edition, 1992).

released that strengthens and prepares the butterfly's wings for flight. So it is for us Christians. If it were possible for us to be cut free from some confrontational issues, it would deny us a key part of growing up in God. Persecution is therefore a natural response to right living.

Persecution is also personal. The hardships we experience are often tailor-made to suit us. God forms and administers our troubles to fit us exactly. As Bob Mumford put it once, "God fixes a fix to fix you, and if you unfix the fix before you're fixed, he'll send another fix to fix you."[73] At the same time, it is comforting to remember that God knows your limits and "will not let you be tempted beyond what you can bear" (1 Corinthians 10:13). Another comforting thought is that persecution doesn't last forever – "though now for a little while you may be distressed by trials and suffer temptations" (1 Peter 1:6, AMP). The fire, pruning hook, flail and rod are "tutors and governors" that bring us to maturity (Galatians 4:2, KJV), if we are "exercised thereby" – that is, if we learn the intended lesson from them (Hebrews 12:11).

In times of trouble, we need to remember that persecution can accomplish in us things that blessing never could.

"We know that all things work together for good to them that love God, to them who are called according to his purpose" (Romans 8:28, KJV). The winepress is integral to producing new wine. The crucible is essential for purifying gold. The pruning hook is needed for procuring fruit. In a similar way, persecution is beneficial to us. The attitude of Joshua and

---

73. *New Wine Magazine*, November 1979, Vol. 11, No.10 (Christian Growth Ministries, 1979).

Caleb was to view conflict as a means of growing rather than groaning. When faced with literal giants, they said: "They are bread for us" (Numbers 14:9, KJV). They saw impending conflict as the nourishment that produces maturity.

Enemy Territory

Twenty-first-century Christians are having to realize more and more that we live in enemy territory. "We know," writes the apostle John, "that the whole world is under the control of the evil one" (1 John 5:19). By the world, John means global systems and societies governed by the kingdom of darkness (John 14:30). The material world is not evil of itself; rather, the systems or governments that oversee it are influenced and manipulated by dark spiritual powers (Ephesians 6:12). Conversely, the psalmist declares, "The earth is the LORD's, and everything in it, the world, and all who live in it" (Psalm 24:1). Like it or not, we're at war. The whole world is involved in a dispute, a question of ownership, an issue of sovereignty. We are either for God and against Satan, or for Satan and against God. Satan is earth's illegal squatter and as such needs to be ousted from the lives of unregenerate people.

God's kingdom and Satan's are diametrically opposed; they are as different as day and night, life and death. Paul expresses this cosmic conflict and its opposing factions in two questions: "What do righteousness and wickedness have in common? Or what fellowship can light have with darkness?" (2 Corinthians 6:14). The answer is, of course, "Nothing!"

This world is a theatre of war and the conflict is an issue of sovereignty. It has been that way since God declared His intention in the Garden of Eden: "I will put enmity between you and the woman, and between your offspring and hers; he will crush your head, and you will strike his heel" (Genesis 3:15).

Every Christian is a conscript in this battle, for there is no neutrality. Ruth Paxson writes, "The immediate object in the conflict is the redemption and reconciliation of the human race ruined through sin. The ultimate object is the restoration of God to undivided sovereignty over all his universe; in other words, the rule of the kingdom of God."[74]

Read the Small Print!

Drawing His description of Christian character to a close, Jesus begins to put the final touches to His masterpiece. Matthew 5:11-12 further define what Jesus said in verse 10: "Blessed . . . enviably fortunate and spiritually prosperous [that is, in the state in which one enjoys and finds satisfaction in God's favour and salvation, regardless of his outward conditions], are those who are persecuted for righteousness' sake (for being and doing right), for theirs is the kingdom of heaven" (AMP). This eighth Be-Attitude, strategically placed as it is, sums up all that has gone before. What Jesus is saying is this:

"When all these Christian characteristics become evident in your life, the result will be persecution, insults, false accusations and people ostracizing you."

In most contracts, this kind of clause would be tucked away in the small print so as not to discourage the prospective buyer. But as William Barclay writes, "One of the outstanding qualities of Jesus was his sheer honesty. He never left men in any doubt what would happen to them if they chose to follow

---

74. Ruth Paxson, *Life on the Highest Plane* (Moody Press, 1978).

him. He was clear that he had come 'not to make life easy, but to make men great.'[75]

Although few of us will ever be called upon to endure the suffering of Ridley and Latimer, our angle of approach to both physical and verbal abuse should follow their example. We are to respond positively to opposition, not react against it. This is an attitude we ignore at our cost. Because the kingdom of God is diametrically opposed to the kingdom of this world – spiritually, morally and behaviourally – persecution is inevitable. The effect of these eight attitudes working together is potential persecution.

Step by step, the first three Be-Attitudes teach us *to rely on God*. Then, having taken our fill of righteousness, we are prepared *to relate to others*. But beware, doing right can result in persecution. Dr Martyn Lloyd-Jones writes, "If you try to imitate Christ, the world will praise you; if you become Christlike it will hate you."[76]

Sons of the Flame

Some people think of Christianity as the "great escape", a prepaid ticket to heaven in which life is merely a departure lounge. Such an idea is of course wrong. If we invite people to receive Christ without telling them the cost, we are not preaching the Good News of the Kingdom. We are instead giving a watered-down gospel that attracts people on the basis of need. This produces an evangelical subculture that views the world with suspicion. This mindset says, "This world is not my home; I'm just a-passing through. And the quicker we get through bandit territory the better!"

---

75. William Barclay, *The Daily Study Bible* (St Andrew Press, 1978).
76. Martyn Lloyd-Jones, *Studies in the Sermon on the Mount* (IVP, 1971).

At last, the Church is beginning to emerge, albeit tentatively, from her self-imposed exile.

The balance between being in the world and not of it is being addressed. The Church is waking up to the truth that heaven's purposes are to be ultimately harmonized with those of earth. An evangelical escape theology is giving way to a true understanding of the gospel of the Kingdom. Bringing in God's rule is costly. As Jesus told His followers: "Any of you who does not give up everything he has cannot be my disciple" (Luke 14:33).

Paul's prayer for the Philippians gives us yet another insight into his attitude to persecution: "Not having a righteousness of my own that comes from the law, but that which is through faith in Christ – the righteousness that comes from God and is by faith. I want to know Christ and the power of his resurrection and the fellowship of sharing in his sufferings, becoming like him in his death" (Philippians 3:9-10).

Paul, in effect, says this: "Whatever the cost or the consequences in terms of this life, I want to embrace it as Jesus did. I want to be an overcomer and not just to party through life. I want to determine in my heart to bring in God's government whatever the cost!"

Jim Elliot, one of five missionaries martyred in the Ecuador jungle in 1956, displayed the same kind of attitude. During his college days at Wheaton, Illinois, he wrote: "He makes his ministers a flame of fire. Am I ignitable? God deliver me from the dread asbestos of 'other things.' Saturate me with the oil of the Spirit that I may be a flame. But flame is transient, often short-lived. Canst thou bear this, my soul – short life? In me there dwells the Spirit of the Great Short-lived, whose zeal for God's house consumed him. 'Make me Thy Fuel, Flame of God.'"[77]

In his words to Job, Eliphaz made a profound statement about persecution: "Man is born to trouble as surely as sparks fly upward" (Job 5:7). The Hebrew word from which we get the English word "sparks" was translated by one man as "son of the flame". What better way is there to characterize the children of God than "sons of the flame"?

Just like Shadrach, Meshach and Abednego, our stand for righteousness is likely to elicit either verbal or physical persecution. But we are "convinced that neither death nor life, neither angels nor demons, neither the present nor the future, nor any powers, neither height nor depth, nor anything else in all creation, will be able to separate us from the love of God that is in Christ Jesus our Lord" (Romans 8:38-39).

Positive ID

You would think that someone who is merciful, pure in heart and a peacemaker would be loved by everyone, but the opposite is true. Paul, a prisoner in Rome, reminds Timothy: "Persecution is inevitable for those who are determined to live really Christian lives" (2 Timothy 3:12, JBP). The idealist view of Christian living in many people's thinking is a peace-loving, pleasant, unprovocative, easy-going, non-aggressive cruise through the warm waters of life. Nothing could be further from the truth. Jesus Himself said, "Do not suppose that I have come to bring peace to the earth. I did not come to bring peace, but a sword" (Matthew 10:34). Previously, when commissioning the Twelve, He indicated that "brother will betray brother to death ... All men will hate you because of me" (Matthew 10:21, 22).

---

77. Elisabeth Elliot, *Through Gates of Splendor* (Tyndale, 1981).

Christianity means warfare, and kingdom life involves conflict.

Yet it is a battle with a difference, for we fight in the light of a victory already won. Christians wear the laurels (crowns) of victory ahead of time. Jesus has accomplished for us the victory on the beachhead of Calvary. Our job is to mop up various pockets of resistance. Calvary was our D-Day; the second coming of Jesus Christ will be our VE-Day.

How can we maintain a positive attitude to opposition? Is it possible to regard the persecuted as "enviably fortunate and spiritually prosperous"? Since God's declaration of war, His servants have suffered. Abel was persecuted by his brother Cain. Moses suffered the insults of his people. David suffered at the hands of Saul. Elijah suffered, as did Jeremiah. Daniel "so distinguished himself . . . by his exceptional qualities" that others "tried to find grounds for charges against [him] . . . but they were unable to do so . . . because he was trustworthy and neither corrupt nor negligent" (Daniel 6:3-5). Yet he suffered, not for being difficult, but for righteousness' sake. He was oppressed for doing what was right. The apostles also suffered, not because they were difficult, but simply because they were righteous. Jesus showed us the perfect angle of approach to persecution: "When they hurled their insults at him, he did not retaliate . . . Instead, he entrusted himself to him who judges justly" (1 Peter 2:23). Read *Fox's Book of Martyrs* and you will see how righteous people suffered at the hands of religious people. The Covenanters, the Protestant Fathers, leaders of the Evangelical Awakening in the 18th century and men like Hudson Taylor all suffered, not because they were difficult or objectionable, but because they were living right.

The remarkable quality that shines through all these dark episodes is the attitude to affliction of the people concerned.

The New Testament continually talks in terms of "being counted worthy to share in Christ's sufferings". Paul described this to the Philippians as "the fellowship of sharing in his sufferings" (Philippians 3:10). Peter puts it like this:

"Now, dear friends of mine. I beg you not to be unduly alarmed at the fiery ordeals which come to test your faith, as though this were some abnormal experience. You should be glad, because it means that you are sharing in Christ's sufferings . . . If you are reproached for being Christ's followers, that is a cause for joy, for you can be sure that God's Spirit of glory is resting upon you. But take care that none of your number suffers as a murderer, or a thief, a rogue or a busybody! If he suffers as a Christian, he has nothing to be ashamed of and may glorify God by confessing Christ's name." (1 Peter 4:12-16, JBP)

"Even if you should suffer for the sake of righteousness, you are blessed" (1 Peter 3:14). Why is it a blessing? Because to suffer for righteousness' sake is to be identified with Jesus. Persecution is viewed in the New Testament as evidence of association. Jesus follows on from His discourse on the true vine and its branches by reminding His disciples, "If the world hates you, keep in mind that it hated me first . . . Remember the words I spoke to you: 'No servant is greater than his master.' If they persecuted me, they will persecute you also . . . They will treat you this way because of my name" (John 15:18-21).

Pressures, problems and persecution are all a part of life. Yet when they are the result of a righteous lifestyle, we can rejoice because persecution is evidence that we are acting just like Jesus. The Pharisees hated Jesus because of His absolute holiness. A disciple is expected to be like his master, and the son is to bear a family resemblance. As sons of God we must therefore have an attitude that expects opposition. In fact, Jesus warned His followers: "Woe to you when all men speak well of you, for that is how their fathers treated the false prophets" (Luke 6:26). If all we know is favour from the world, we are not living a righteous life, a life modelled after and conformed to the image of Jesus.

We can have a positive attitude to persecution when we realize that the world will hate us, exclude us, insult us and reject us because we are like Jesus. When we are persecuted for righteousness' sake, it is a sign that the world associates us with Jesus. Remember, the apostles, having been flogged and ordered not to speak in the name of Jesus, left the Sanhedrin court "rejoicing because they had been counted worthy of suffering disgrace for the Name" (Acts 5:17-42).

For Righteousness' Sake!

We can have a positive attitude to persecution that is "because of righteousness", but there is no virtue in being persecuted for being foolish, or for having an irritating personality. Peter makes it clear that we must never be persecuted "as a murderer, or a thief, or any sort of criminal; or as a mischief-maker (a meddler) in the affairs of others – infringing on their rights" (1 Peter 4:15, AMP). Let's look at these:

- Murderer – someone who makes an attack on another person's life. This could include the seeds of murder, such as hatred, resentment, or the assassination of a person's character. If we engage in this, we can expect to be unpopular.

- Thief – to steal is to abuse a person's possessions. Included in seeds of theft are the stealing of another person's time or the taking of praise due to another. If we exhibit this sort of character, we can expect to be ostracized.

- Meddler – someone who interferes in a person's responsibilities – a busybody. Offering unwise, untimely or unwelcome help. If we do this, we can expect trouble.

If we suffer for any of these issues, the persecution that follows is thoroughly justified and deserved. It is all completely avoidable. But if we are "insulted because of the name of Christ", we should rejoice that this is an acknowledgement of our state and standing in Christ. We are therefore provoked to rejoice that we "bear that name" (1 Peter 4:14-17). Positive identification allows us to embrace a positive approach to persecution.

The Oxford Dictionary defines the verb "persecute" as "to pursue with enmity and ill-treatment; harass; worry; importune". Such harassment may range from verbal to emotional abuse and may also extend to the physical abuse of one's property or person. Some Christians today are imprisoned for their faith. Others are ostracized by their peers, colleagues, family or relatives. But for the majority of Christians in the West, the persecution is of a verbal nature: insults, false rumours, gossip, slander and libel.

The New Testament word translated "persecute" is translated by some as "to drive away". Kittel, however, suggests a two-fold idea: first, "to ride, to march, to set in rapid motion"; and second, "to expel, to accuse".[78] This is seen in the words of Pharaoh pursuing the children of Israel: "The enemy boasted, 'I will pursue, I will overtake them. I will divide the spoils; I will gorge myself on them. I will draw my sword and my hand will destroy them'" (Exodus 15:9). Such situations are the result of a clash of the kingdoms

Taking versions of Luke 6:22 (the Amplified Bible and J.B. Phillips), we know that the world will "despise and hate us, exclude and excommunicate us (as disreputable), slander us and reject all that we stand for, because you are loyal to the Son of Man". Kingdom living involves conflict. But approached correctly, such persecution can be a means of rejoicing. We are not to allow resentment or a desire for retaliation to take root. Instead, we are to "be glad ... and jump for joy – your reward in heaven is magnificent. For that is exactly how their fathers treated the prophets."

Numbers clearly are significant to God. In biblical numerology, the number 7 is the number of completion or perfection, while 8 is the number of new beginnings. This eighth Be-Attitude could be said to speak of the beginning of a new era. This attitude, climaxing all that has gone before, has to do with our angle of approach to pressure, (see page 59).

Richard Wurmbrand was held for fourteen years in Communist prisons. For almost three years, he was kept in a room three paces by three, thirty-five feet under the ground,

---

78. Gerhard Kittel (ed.) and Gerhard Friedrich (ed.), *Theological Dictionary of the New Testament*, Vol. 2 (Eerdmans, 1976) pp. 229-230.

with only a tube for air. Despite being beaten, tortured and drugged, his captors could not force him to confess to the false allegations brought against him. He writes:

"The Communists believe that happiness comes from material satisfaction; but alone in my cell, cold, hungry and in rags, I danced for joy every night . . . Sometimes I was so filled with joy that I felt I would burst if I did not give it expression. I remembered the words of Jesus: 'Blessed are you when men come to hate you, when they exclude you from their company and reproach you and cast out your name as evil on account of the Son of Man. Rejoice in that day and leap for joy!' I told myself: 'I've carried out only half this command. I've rejoiced, but that is not enough. Jesus says clearly that we must also leap.'

"When next the guard peered through the spy-hole, he saw me springing about my cell. His orders must have been to distract anyone who showed signs of breakdown, for he padded off and returned with some food from the staff room: a hunk of bread, some cheese and sugar. As I took them I remembered how the verse in St Luke went on: 'Rejoice in that day and leap for joy – for behold your reward is great.' It was a very large piece of bread: more than a week's ration.

"I rarely allowed a night to pass without dancing, from then on, although I was never paid for it again. I made up songs and sang them softly to myself and danced to my own music . . . It was a manifestation of joy like the dance of David, a holy sacrifice offered before the altar of the Lord. I did not mind if my captors thought I was mad, for I had discovered a beauty in Christ which I had not known before.

"Sometimes I saw visions . . . Then the cell was full of light . . . Another night I became aware of a great throng of angels moving slowly through the darkness towards my bed. As they approached they sang a song of love."[79]

If only this could be our attitude to the pressures of life – to have this kind of mindset when approaching those who ostracize us or abuse us verbally or physically. Surely what the enemy meant for our detriment could then be turned to our advantage.

Pure Gold

Perhaps the best documented example of pressure, trials and testing is the story of Job. In his most arduous moment, he cried: "He knows the way that I take; when he has tested me, I shall come forth as gold" (Job 23:10).

God uses only pure gold that has been refined in the fire (Revelation 3:18). Although our redemption is complete, and an internal change has taken place, we still have the dross of wrong thinking to bring to the surface and remove. For centuries, people have been trying to make gold from lead, but without success. The reason is that there needs to be a change in the molecular structure. Our molecular structure has been changed at the cross, but the heat of trials and other pressures brings to the surface the negative as well as the positive.

It is reckoned by most goldsmiths that beaten gold is not only stronger but also of greater value than poured gold. Interestingly, most of the golden instruments in the Tabernacle of Moses were made from beaten gold.

Our attitude needs to be this: "I must be precious and useful if God is allowing me to go through this fiery trail."

---

79. Richard Wurmbrand, *In God's Underground* (Living Sacrifice Book Co., re-issue edition, 2004).

Remember that God never leaves His children to go through the fire alone; He is always there with them. He has a vested interest in the gold.

Adversity can mean success to those who maintain a redemptive, rather than adversarial attitude. John Bunyan wrote *Pilgrim's Progress* in Bedford jail. Luther translated the Bible while confined in Wartburg Castle. Beethoven was almost totally deaf and burdened with sorrow when he produced his greatest works. Be it the cave, wilderness, pit or prison, it is difficult to find a well-known Bible character who did not first have to attend the school of persecution before emerging as a great leader.

In *Awake, My Heart*, Sidlow Baxter writes, "What is the difference between an obstacle and an opportunity? Our attitude toward it. Every opportunity has a difficulty and every difficulty has an opportunity."[80]

---

80. J. Sidlow Baxter, Awake, *My Heart* (Zondervan, 1960).

GROUP DISCUSSION AND PERSONAL APPLICATION GUIDE

Group Discussion:

- Do you think that persecution for Christians is more, or less, likely in the 21st century?

- When was the last time you were persecuted for your faith?

- Is there a difference between being "picked on" by non-believers and "picked out"?

- Can you as a group spend some time in prayer for the persecuted church around the world?

Personal Application:

- Would people pick you out in your workplace, college, home, or neighbourhood as a known follower of Jesus Christ?

When it comes to Personal Application we would encourage you to involve a "Spiritual Summiteer" (see page 37) so as to give yourself some level of accountability and guide you on your ongoing journey.

CONCLUSION

CHICKENS FLAP,
EAGLES FLY

"Attitudes are the librarian of our past, the speaker
of our present and the prophet of our future."
John Maxwell[81]

An elderly couple who had lived in the same village community all their lives decided to go globetrotting. Since it was their first time outside their native Yorkshire, they were keen to learn from the experiences of others. On hearing that their trip included a first night stopover in down-town New York, their friends made the couple aware of the dangers of inner-city night life for unsuspecting visitors. They told stories of murder, mugging and mayhem. Even before the couple's first night on American soil, these stories had set off a chain reaction of fear in the two tourists.

Once they had arrived in New York, they settled themselves into their hotel room and decided to go and view some of the sights. When they reached the hotel lobby, the lady realized she had forgotten her handbag.

"You carry on, and I'll go back to the room," she said. She retrieved her bag from the room and began to make her way back to the hotel entrance.

She entered an empty lift and was joined by a tall, handsome man with a large dog. While trying hard not to look at them, she watched in terror as her only way of escape closed automatically in front of her.

81, John C. Maxwell, *The Winning Attitude: Your Key to Personal Success* (Thomas Nelson, 1993).

The silent, slow descent of the lift seemed almost unbearable. With every passing floor the tension grew. Now the dog was becoming restless.

Why didn't I heed those warnings and avoid New York? Why didn't I stay in my Yorkshire village?

Suddenly, the silence was shattered by a shout.

"Get down! Lie down ... on the floor!"

The elderly lady dropped to the ground. What she feared most was surely about to happen. At any moment, she would be assaulted.

What she hadn't realized was that the words were actually meant for the dog. The friendly and somewhat amused gentleman helped her to her feet. Apologizing for the misunderstanding, the young man left her to go her own way.

When the couple came to check out of the hotel the next day, they found that their bill had been paid by the unknown man in the lift, who had also left a bouquet of flowers.

The name of the mystery philanthropist?

Singer Lionel Richie!

This story highlights the power that our attitudes have over our behaviour. The lady in the lift had developed an attitude of suspicion. When she found herself in a confined space with a dog and a man, her attitude reinforced her belief that the city she was in was a dangerous place. This activated her pre-existing fears and led her to misinterpret the man's command to his dog, causing her to throw herself on the floor in a panic! All this was rooted in wrong attitudes, generated by the stories she had heard.

Like the gearbox of a car, our attitudes, once engaged, take us on a course of action that is either progressive or regressive, favourable or unfavourable.

Put another way, attitudes are predetermined patterns of thinking that affect the way we act or react to a given situation. Faced with the same set of circumstances, one person will act in one way, while another will act differently. One person will smile at the dog as it lies down, the other will hurl herself to the floor in terror. It's all a question of attitude.

Our Angle of Approach

On a winter day in 1903, in the Outer Banks of North Carolina, two unknown brothers from Ohio changed history. The age of flight had begun with the first heavier-than-air, powered machine carrying a pilot.

What, in terms of their aviation adventure, did the Wright Brothers get wrong?

Nothing!

In an age when many were seeking to overcome the law of gravity, Wilbur and Orville Wright approached things differently, relying instead on the law of aerodynamics. While others were trying to develop more powerful engines that could break free of earth's gravitational pull, the Wright brothers looked for ways to alter and adjust an aircraft's *attitude*. Learning to control the aircraft's angle of approach was the crucial and often missing factor in achieving successful flight.

Having read some material in preparation for my one and only flying lesson, I was struck by one simple equation explaining flight:

POWER + ATTITUDE = PERFORMANCE

Orville and Wilbur understood that no matter how much power a plane has in terms of lift, without the correct angle, the law of gravity will never give way to the law of aerodynamics.

The Wright brothers got it right. They placed greater emphasis on controlling the attitude than searching for more power.[82]

Taking Control

If the component parts of our attitudes are beliefs, feelings and action, then simply addressing our actions will create little in terms of lasting change. We can strongly dictate to people how they should behave, but as any parent will tell you, the effects are short-term. Consider the little boy who, when he was asked repeatedly by his parents to sit down, initially refused. The precocious four-year-old eventually submitted, but not without saying, "I may be sitting down on the outside, but I'm still standing up on the inside!"

We can punish a person for their misbehaviour but unless they alter their angle-of-approach-to-life, they will perpetuate their former practices. What many of us would like to know is how we can challenge and change our beliefs and so alter our attitudes.

Attitudes are fixed and therefore not easily changed. Like an old, familiar jacket they become comfortable. To change our attitudes not only means admitting we are wrong but involves us having to do some work. To remove the external effects of an attitude, we must first deal with our deep-seated beliefs. It is in our minds that all attitudinal problems are resolved. Alter a person's mindset and you will transform a negative thought pattern into a positive one. I'm not speaking here of the power of positive thinking. Nor am I teaching a kind of metaphysics of mind over matter. There is only one effective way of changing deep-seated attitudes – through the power of the gospel of Jesus Christ.

---

82. David McCullough, *The Wright Brothers* (Simon & Schuster, reprint edition, 2016).

But what exactly is this power that can instigate such a life-changing process? It is the Word of God. I know of no other instrument that can penetrate the thick skin of human resistance and bring change.

God's Word can cut through the scar tissue of past experiences and bring healing.

It can lay an axe to our wrong beliefs and instil new ones. As the Bible teaches, "The Word of God is living and active. Sharper than any double-edged sword, it penetrates even to dividing soul and spirit, joints and marrow; it judges the thoughts and attitudes of the heart" (Hebrews 4:12). It is the application of the truth of God's Word that will bring a lasting remedy to wrong attitudes.

Own Up, They Belong to You!

When we acknowledge wrong attitudes, this requires that we take responsibility and resolve to change. Our tendency is to justify ourselves. "I can't help it. It's my temperament." "It's not my fault. My parents were just the same." Such attempts to intellectualize or minimize our wrong thinking is not the basis for our release.

The first step to implementing change is to admit that we ourselves are responsible for our unhealthy thinking. We need to acknowledge that faulty attitudes belong to us; they are in our heads because we have allowed them entrance, and therefore we cannot blame others for their influence on our thinking. We must choose to be responsible for our own deep-seated mindsets otherwise the whole process of change becomes much more protracted and painful than it ever needs to be. As Bob Mumford comments, "If we decide early in the game that we are going to embrace truth whenever we meet it, no matter what the cost, we will find it much easier to deal with each test as it comes along. Buying truth on the instalment plan is always more expensive."[83]

The person who hates authority often accuses others of being authoritarian. The truth of the matter may well be that the individual concerned has an attitude problem because of a strict disciplinarian upbringing, leading them to mistrust people in authority, and unjustly to accuse them of the misuse of power. This is all a bit like the old lady who rushed out into the garden on a warm summer's day, frantically retrieving her washing from the line before the threatened storm. Then she remembered she was wearing her sunglasses and that the threatening skies were the result of her lenses. "Everything looked so dark," she said, "I was certain it was about to rain!" Like her, we often react to situations in a certain way because of the lenses we have learned to use.

The apostle Paul encouraged the Philippian believers to exercise the same attitude. He wrote: "All of us who are mature should take such a view of things. And if on some point you think differently, that too God will make clear to you" (Philippians 3:15). The New American Standard Bible translates the same verse as: "Let us therefore, as many as are perfect, have this attitude; and if in anything you have a different attitude, God will reveal that also to you."

Attitudes are our personal perspective, the lenses through which we see the episodes of life. As such they affect the way we act or react.

---

83. Bob Mumford, "Below the Bottom Line", *New Wine Magazine* (Christian Growth Ministries).

Take a Risk: Be Radical!

The Bible teaches that the basic key to all behavioural change is repentance – "a change of mind leading to a change of behaviour". Since most emotional and behavioural problems issue from unhealthy attitudes, it is futile to treat the behavioural symptoms without dealing with their cause. That would be like taking the bulb out of a dashboard when it flashes to alert us that the oil of the car needs changing.

Biblical repentance involves a change of thinking which in turn results in a change of behaviour. Changing our thinking requires that we begin to view an issue from God's perspective and behave accordingly. The prodigal son's way back to a right relationship with his father began when "he came to his senses" (Luke 15:17). In the same way, salvation is a restoration of the whole person, a coming alive to God that begins with repentance (a change of thinking) and brings us into wholeness of life.

The prodigal's return resulted first and foremost in a restoration of his identity as his father's son. His father's gift of the best robe (Luke 15:22) was a sign of reconciliation and a means of identifying him publicly as his son, not his servant. The son returned home feeling thoroughly condemned, locked into a devalued view of himself. The best he could hope for was servanthood. Instead, he received a public and unmistakable demonstration that he was once again a part of the family.

New birth re-establishes the repentant individual to a right relationship with the Father. The indwelling power of the Holy Spirit enables people to reflect on who they are in Christ Jesus – sons and daughters of God who serve Him willingly. The speedy response ordered by the father of the prodigal not only restored his son's estimation of who he was, but also reinstated his birth right – his authority. This was indicated by the signet ring that the father ordered his servants to present to his son. In the Old Testament, Pharaoh gave a restored Joseph "his signet ring ... [and] dressed him in robes of fine linen" to signify the authority invested in him (Genesis 41:42). In the same way, the father of the prodigal gave his son a ring. This ring told the son who he was (identity) and what he had (authority). This attitudinal change therefore involves not only a recognition of who we are in Christ Jesus but also an understanding of our God-given power and authority. As sons, we have a right to rule – the power to rule ourselves as well as our circumstances. We are empowered to live free from unhealthy beliefs that lead to wrong behaviour.

With a restored sense of identity and authority, the prodigal was also given a new direction, a new destiny. The haphazard, aimless drudgery that marked his life on the pig farm was not the destiny to which he had been born. Neither is it the kind of lifestyle God has in mind for those who are born again into the household of faith. The Damascus-road experience caused Saul to ask two fundamental questions: "Who art thou, Lord?" and "What wilt thou have me to do?" (Acts 9:5-6, KJV).

To the Christian, the gospel of the Kingdom is an issue of lordship as well as a challenge of ownership.

Acting on Information Received

Peter writes this:

> "His divine power has given us everything we need for life and godliness through our knowledge of him who has called us by his own glory and goodness. Through these he has given us his very great and precious promises,

so that through them you may participate in the divine nature and escape the corruption in the world caused by evil desires." (2 Peter 1:3-4)

By receiving God's Word in faith, we can align our thinking with God's. Just as a soldier puts on his helmet as protection for the coming battle, so the Christian is to apply the truth, not merely appreciate and acknowledge it. In donning "the helmet of salvation" (Ephesians 6:17), we apply God's truth to our thoughts and align our thoughts to God's truth. Putting the same principle another way, Paul writes to the Christians in Rome: "Count yourselves dead" (Romans 6:11). The King James Version puts it, "Reckon . . . yourselves to be dead." What is he saying? Simply this: "Reckon on the fact that you have died to the past and live according to God's Word in the present." Changing our thinking requires us to die to past attitudes and live in the light of God's Be-Attitudes.

The word "count" or "reckon" is an accountancy term that means to recognize in reality what we have available to us. Although I may think I have nothing, it is what I really have that counts. I literally count the money I have in my pocket and I live according to what is truly available to me. I live by facts, not feelings, nor by wishful thinking.

The apostle Paul tells you to count on the fact that Christ has died and that you died with him. This is an historical, eternal and present fact that cannot be altered. "He died to sin [ending His relation to it] once for all, and the life that He lives, He is living to God [in unbroken fellowship with Him]. Even so consider yourselves also dead to sin and your relation to it broken" (Romans 6:10-11, AMP).

The redemptive work of Christ is a truth to be applied, not merely admired.

We do not live free by the so-called power of positive thinking, or the repeating of empty phrases, or a mere mental assent. Instead, we build our lives on divine truth revealed by the Holy Spirit and established in our innermost beings. Paul wrote to the Christians in Rome: "We know that our old self was crucified with him" (Romans 6:6). Each of us needs to appropriate the truth, "and the truth will set [us] free" (John 8:32).

Breaking the Mould

Breaking the habit of a long-established attitude is a very real possibility through Christ. The mindset that refuses to move beyond well-worn tracks of past hurts hampers its own progress towards attitudinal change. We need to experience the renewing power of the Holy Spirit, break out of the past and live in the fulness of God's will today. We alone are responsible for adjusting our thinking so that our thoughts are aligned with God's. If we deny all knowledge of our actions or reactions we are like ostriches, burying our heads in the sand. We are each answerable for our attitudes. It is no use blaming our behaviour on the past – on our upbringing or peer pressure. A born-again child of God has what it takes to overcome every historical hindrance and to live victoriously. We need to collaborate with the indwelling power of the Holy Spirit to help us mirror ourselves in the truth of God's Word and break free from the negative and faulty images we hold of ourselves.

The little-known Old Testament character called Jabez was branded with a name that sounds like the Hebrew word for "pain". Who can tell what disabling effect such a name had on his early childhood and then later as an adult? Words have an immeasurable effect, especially on young minds, emotionally and socially. Tragically, parents today still name their children with little thought. What an agony it must have been for children to grow up in the 20th century with names like *John Will Fail*, *Welcome Baby Darling* and *Justin Pink*! Other children, through no fault of their own, have become emotionally disabled through unwise naming.

Jabez, in contrast, refused his mother's naming. He cried out to God, "Oh, that you would bless me and enlarge my territory! Let your hand be with me and keep me from harm so that I will be free from pain." The Bible says, "And God granted his request" (1 Chronicles 4:10).

No limitation was going to inhibit this man of God. He took hold of his inheritance and became a winner.

Cabbage-patch Mentality

The apostle Paul says this in Romans 12:2 (AMP): "Do not be conformed to this world . . . But be transformed (changed) by the [entire] renewal of your mind [by its new ideals and its new attitude] so that you may prove [for yourselves] what is the good and acceptable and perfect will of God." The Greek word translated "transformed" is also used to describe the transfiguration of Jesus in Matthew 17:1-13. In his second letter to the church in Corinth, Paul speaks of the spiritual process by which the Christian is "being transformed into [Jesus'] likeness with ever-increasing glory, which comes from the Lord, who is the Spirit" (2 Corinthians 3:18). Through the Spirit, our attitudes can experience a transfiguration. They can become luminous with the glory of God's truth.

From this Greek word we also get the English word "metamorphosis". To the entomologist, this word conveys the transformation of a caterpillar through the chrysalis stage into a beautiful butterfly. Through the process of metamorphosis, the insect changes not only its form and appearance but its habits and way of life. The same can be said of those who profess to be living under God's rule (1 Corinthians 6:9-11). If the butterfly is to move from its former cabbage-patch existence and survive in the totally new environment for which it is now well suited, it must change its angle of approach to life. Likewise, through the cross of Christ, we have been changed, are being changed and will be further changed. But if this middle ground of "being changed" is not to become a quagmire of mediocrity, we need to learn to think differently. Our attitudes must change. God has fitted us to fly, to "reign in life through the one man, Jesus Christ" (Romans 5:17). We are to live above our circumstances, not beneath them, and we are to rule in life knowing that "God raised us up with Christ and seated us with him in the heavenly realms" (Ephesians 2:6).

If you want to find a new formula for life that will take the hassle out of home life and the drudgery out of work, then develop a new and right attitude, founded on what God says, revealed through His Word and by His Holy Spirit. Focus your thinking on godly ways of thinking and fix your mind on whatever is true, noble, right, pure, lovely and admirable (Philippians 4:8). Such thinking creates a wall, a protective barrier of peace, that will maintain your joy as well as guard your life.

It's not that Jesus needs to do any more for *us*, but He does have to do a lot more *in* us.

This is what the Bible means by being "transformed by the renewing of your mind" (Romans 12:2). J.B. Phillips' version puts it this way: "Don't let the world around you squeeze you into its mould, but let God remake you so that your whole attitude of mind is changed." Attitudinal change is the result of the Holy Spirit interacting with our spirit, changing our beliefs in line with God's way of thinking. It is therefore how you respond to God's grace in your life that makes attitudinal change possible. Here are a few keys for you to adopt when considering a change of attitude:

- Humble yourself (James 4:6-10; 1 Peter 5:5-11)
- Draw near to God (Hebrews 4:16)
- Ask for help
- Resist negative thoughts
- Don't buy the lie (2 Corinthians 10:4-5)
- Put yourself under the authority of God's Word
- Meditate on God's positive attributes
- Apply the truth (Ephesians 6:14; Matthew 4:1-10; 1 John 4:4)

Giving Birth to the New Me

Any midwife or mother-to-be knows the importance and implications of a change of attitude. The position of a baby prior to delivery is known as the "foetal attitude" and is vital to the birth process. The angle at which the unborn child presents him or herself determines the degree of ease which mother and child will experience during birth.

The implications of a so-called "bad attitude baby" are well known. Any deviation from what is termed normal can result in a difficult labour. An abnormal attitude can sometimes obstruct the process of labour. Although the majority of "bad attitude babies" change their angle of approach unaided and so enter the world normally, those who maintain a bad attitude increase the risk of trauma to both themselves and their mothers.

We may have high hopes and great ambitions for our future, but unless we maintain a right and good attitude, we will have difficulty in bringing to birth God's vision for our lives and we run the risk of aborting His dream. Think of Solomon; because of a wrong attitude, he had the kingdom torn from him (1 Kings 11:11). Think of Caleb; through "a different attitude", he, along with Joshua, managed to achieve his goal in life (Numbers 14:24). Shouldn't we also want to maintain a healthy attitude to fulfil our God-given destiny?

On Your Bike!

A few years back, when I was working as a carpenter, I was involved in a kitchen refit in the north of England at the home of a keen road cyclist. The house was so littered with the paraphernalia of his chosen sport that there was little room for anything else. I was fascinated to know more about a hobby for which he clearly lived and breathed. I asked his wife how her husband managed to pursue his interest amidst the harsh realities of a Yorkshire winter. She answered, "Well, each Sunday morning without fail he's up at the crack of dawn and dressed in his riding gear ready to go."

"Even when there's snow on the ground?"

"Oh, yes."

I was impressed. Such dedication to a sport during the bitter cold of a Yorkshire winter is, to say the least, commendable.

Seeing the look of admiration on my face, she was quick to correct any misconceptions I had. "Oh, no, you don't understand. Once he puts on his cycling gear, he brings his bike into the living room, puts on the gas fire, gets out his cycling magazines and sits down in the chair to dream of the day when he can take to the road again."

Jesus has some harsh words in Matthew 25:14-30 for those who, having received, sit back idly awaiting the King's return. His rebuke should awaken us all to the needs of the world. Those who are truly righteous are to feed the hungry, give a drink to the thirsty, open their doors to the stranger, clothe and care for the needy. As someone has said, "An individual has not started living until he can rise above the narrow confines of his individualistic concerns to the broader concerns of all humanity. Every man must decide whether he will walk in the light of creative altruism [regard for others as a principle of action] or the darkness of destructive selfishness. This is the judgment. Life's most persistent and urgent question is, 'What are you doing for others?'"[84]

A former British politician is often misquoted as telling the unemployed "to get on their bikes and look for employment". If we are to take the Be-Attitudes seriously, it's no good putting on our Sunday best and sitting in our living rooms with a Bible on our laps. We need to get out and apply them in the world, however harsh the spiritual winter may feel in our nation at any given time. Christians must break out of bricks and mortar. We must feel the wind and snow outside. Christianity must become incarnated in the ice and blizzards of a cold-hearted world and address the relevant issues of the day. The Church cannot remain silent on such issues as racism, abuse, poverty, homelessness, violence, inner-city crime and social deprivation.

Life's harsh realities must not become no-go areas for the Church. Authentic Christianity belongs in the grit and grime of humanity and the Church needs to decide what sort of world it wants to help to create. The next ten years will decide the shape of the 21st century. They may decide the future of the earth as a habitation for human beings.

---

84. Coretta Scott King, *The Words of Martin Luther King, Jr.* (HarperCollins, 2001).

Attitude Determines Altitude

Have you ever noticed how some people seem to soar above the challenges of life, while others struggle under a cloud of circumstances? The reason for the contrast is simple – attitude. Attitudes are the lenses through which we view life. They colour our thinking and the way we approach people, objects and events. The subject of *Life on the Hill* has been the eight Be-Attitudes taught by Jesus in the Sermon on the Mount. Collectively they lay the foundation for a profoundly Christian worldview. They form a heavenly octave that should resonate with those who see themselves as disciples of Jesus.

These eight angles of approach to everyday life are not just a checklist: they are a rule of life.

While taxiing up and down religious runways, perhaps it is time for us to take the eight opening statements of the Sermon on the Mount seriously. If the "Law of First Mention" has any value, then surely we should take note of Jesus's opening words to His most famous sermon. This is His manifesto for kingdom living.

There comes a moment in the take-off of an aircraft when the law of gravity will give way to the law of aerodynamics. Pulling on the inherent power of those jet engines, the plane that was a few moments earlier taxiing is about to soar. This is what this aircraft was created to do. To be forever parked at the terminal is a terrible waste of this invaluable resource. It was designed to fly.

If the 2020 pandemic has done anything, it has certainly got our attention. Faced with their own mortality, people are trying to think long-term but having to think short-term. For committed followers of Jesus Christ, it's time to stop taxiing around life's runways. It's time to push away from those terminals of people, objects and events that are stopping us doing what God created us for and it's time to pull on the inherent power of God's indwelling Holy Spirit, to surge away from earth's gravitational pull, and to rise to do what God has always intended for us to do.

Why?

Because it's time to soar!

Chickens flap, but eagles fly.

GROUP DISCUSSION AND PERSONAL APPLICATION GUIDE

Group Discussion:

- Has anyone seen someone crash and burn because of an ill-adjusted attitude?
- Of the eight Be-Attitudes, which one do you feel is the most challenging and why?
- How can we stop *Life on the Hill* becoming a visitors' centre rather than a place of residence?

Personal Application:

- What attitude change occurred when you became a Christ follower and are those changes still true?
- If you were asked to journal your journey through *Life on the Hill*, what would you write about each of the following stopping off points?

    Poverty of Spirit

    Mourning

    Meekness

    Hunger and Thirst for Rightness

    Showing Mercy

Pure Motives

Making Peace

Persecution

When it comes to Personal Application we would encourage you to involve a "Spiritual Summiteer" (see page 37) so as to give yourself some level of accountability and guide you on your ongoing journey.

ABOUT THE AUTHOR

Chris Spicer is a leader with over fifty years of experience working with Christian communities and learning centres throughout Europe and North America. Having lived in Portland, Oregon, and Peoria, Illinois, Chris now lives in England. He and his wife Tina have four adult children and eight rock-star grandchildren. Public speaker and published author, Chris's other titles include: *No Perfect Fathers Here*; *JJ & the Big Bend*; and *The Reel Story*.

You can visit his website at spicersink.com, and you can follow him on Twitter, Facebook and Instagram.

Printed in Great Britain
by Amazon